WHEN YOU PRAY

DAILY PRACTICES FOR PRAYERFUL LIVING

Rueben P. Job

When You Pray

Daily Practices for Prayerful Living

Revised Edition

Compiled and edited by
Pamela C. Hawkins

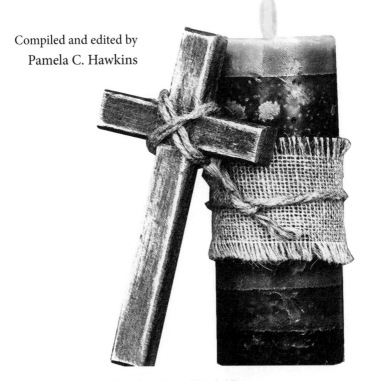

Abingdon Press / Nashville

WHEN YOU PRAY
Daily Practices for Prayerful Living—Revised Edition

1st Edition Copyright © 2009 Abingdon Press
Revised Edition Copyright © 2018 Abingdon Press
All rights reserved.

This book is printed on elemental chlorine-free paper.
Library of Congress Cataloging-in-Publication Data for Revised Edition has been requested.
ISBN 978-1-5018-58536

Library of Congress Cataloging-in-Publication Data for First Edition.
Job, Rueben P.
When you pray : daily practices for prayerful living / Rueben P. Job.
     p. cm.
ISBN 978-1-4267-0266-2 (binding: leather / fine binding/leather - imitation : alk. paper)
1. United Methodist Church (U.S.)--Prayers and devotions. 2. Church year meditations.
3. Common lectionary (1992) I. Title.
BV245.J59 2009
242'.2--dc22
                    2009019708

Scripture quotations unless noted otherwise are taken from the Common English Bible, copyright 2011. Used by permission. All rights reserved.

Scripture quotations marked NRSV are from the New Revised Standard Version Bible, copyright © 1989 National Council of the Churches of Christ in the United States of America. Used by permission. All rights reserved worldwide. http://nrsvbibles.org/

Scripture quotations noted Jerusalem Bible are from *The Jerusalem Bible* © 1966 by Darton, Longman & Todd, Ltd. and Doubleday, a division of Random House, Inc. Reprinted by Permission.

Scripture texts noted NAB in this work are taken from the *New American Bible, revised edition* © 2010, 1991, 1986, 1970 Confraternity of Christian Doctrine, Washington, D.C. and are used by permission of the copyright owner. All Rights Reserved. No part of the New American Bible may be reproduced in any form without permission in writing from the copyright owner.

18 19 20 21 22 23 24 25 26 27 — 10 9 8 7 6 5 4 3 2 1
PRINTED IN THE PEOPLE'S REPUBLIC OF CHINA

User's Guide

Welcome to your personal copy of *When You Pray: Daily Practices for Prayerful Living*. It is designed for all who seek to live faithfully and fully as followers of Jesus Christ, and each part is intended to aid you in your own walk with God. Nothing in the following pages provides a magic formula to nurture your own soul, but all in the following pages is designed to place in your hands ancient and contemporary resources, that when utilized, lead to a closer and life-giving companionship with the One who loves you without limit and desires to dwell within you as a loving and wise guide, companion, and source of strength.

This resource seeks to respond to the needs we all have for a pattern of prayer that is accessible, usable, and adaptable to our diverse life experiences in our contemporary world. What you have in your hands has grown out of my discoveries as I continue to learn how to pray following the pattern of prayer that Jesus has given in the prayer he taught the disciples and in his own prayers recorded in the Gospels.

It is amazing that the disciples did not ask Jesus to teach them how to tell a parable, multiply the loaves, or heal the sick; but they did ask him to teach them how to pray. And when asked, Jesus taught them this simple and complete prayer. And the Lord's Prayer has been our pattern of prayer ever since. The disciples' request and the response of Jesus is more than a subtle reminder of the importance of prayer for them and for us. This brief prayer contains the essential elements of a healthy life of prayer and a healthy relationship with the One to whom we pray.

You may already have a pattern for your daily life of prayer that is serving you well. In that case, you may make more limited use of some of the segments of this design of a pattern for daily prayer. However, if you do not have such a pattern, I encourage you to try the pattern of prayer offered here. Over a period of several months of daily use, you will adapt and adjust it to your own particular needs that will permit it to become your own personal pattern of prayer.

Do not use it as a rule that must be followed to the letter of the law, rather use it as a guide to daily bring you to awareness of God's presence and the table of rich resources provided for your spiritual nourishment and direction. The movements of the Lord's Prayer and the elements of this pattern of prayer for daily use are important, if not essential, to discovering and practicing our own way of living with God. Becoming aware of God's presence, inviting God's intervention, listening for God's voice, making our requests known, offering ourselves to God, and receiving God's blessing are all essential elements in a faithful and fulfilling life with God. Our task is to weave them into the seamless garment of relationship with God that will sustain us in every experience of life and make it possible for us to live at home with God in this world and the next.

Rueben P. Job, 2009
"User's Guide," *When You Pray: Daily Practices for Prayerful Living* (1st Edition)

How to Use This Book

The following paragraphs will introduce you to each of the segments of this book and how they may be used by individuals, families, or small groups. Because we are each different and God is infinite, we should not expect our patterns of prayer to be identical. The important part is to shape and establish a daily pattern of prayer that meets your own personal needs and the needs of your family, small group, or larger community and remains faithful to the prayer that Jesus taught us to use.

In a letter to John Trembath, John Wesley said, "O begin! Fix some part of every day for private exercises. You may acquire the taste which you have not: What is tedious at first, will afterwards be pleasant. Whether you like it or no, read and pray daily. It is for your life: there is no other way. . . . Do justice to your own soul: give it time and means to grow. Do not starve yourself any longer." (John Wesley, *The Works of John Wesley*, 12:254.) His words continue to be good advice.

Week Number The readings are numbered from 1 to 52, guiding you through a year. The first reading begins with Week 1, and you may wish to begin there. If you would like to pray along with the church calendar, the first week also has some Scriptures of the Advent season, a pattern repeated at Lent, Eastertide. A lectionary guide on page 315 lists the weeks associated with each church season. But if you prefer to pray by theme, you will find a list of themes on page 11 from which you may choose in any order.

Theme The theme for each week of the year is drawn from the church calendar, beginning with the season of Advent. But each week also includes readings chosen simply for how they illumine the theme, rather than time of year.

Approaching God with Intention The approach to each time of prayer offers either an opening prayer or Scripture passage that is chosen to help you settle into an intentional time with God.

Practicing Stillness (Indicated each week by the dove icon) After intentionally approaching and entering into this time with God, take a moment to become still and to sit in silence. A few words of instruction are provided to guide you in this time. This is the time to quiet the noise around you and heed the call to "be still, and know that I am God!" (Psalm 46:10 NRSV). *(*Rueben P. Job, *Listen: Praying in a Noisy World*, 17.)

Becoming Aware of God's Presence is a brief Scripture passage for reading and meditation as you make room in your mind and heart to hear and respond to the call of God and to recognize and welcome God's presence in your life, family, or small group.

Inviting God's Intervention is also a brief Scripture or quotation inviting God to act in your life, your family, your small group, the church, and indeed in the whole world.

Listening for God's Voice is a time to seek to open your life more fully to what God is saying to you as an individual, family, or small group. Try to open yourself to hear what a Scripture passage is saying to you and how the message of the essay and quotations inform your walk of faithfulness.

Read the suggested Scripture passage several times, or choose one of the Alternative Readings found in the sidebar. Try to place yourself "beneath" the passage. That is, let the passage address you with its questions and affirmations. "What is God saying to me in this passage?" Permit the passage to be God's living word to you. (Rueben P. Job, *A Guide to Retreat for All God's Shepherds*, 15.)

All of the Scripture suggestions support and enhance the week's theme. Also there are often one or more readings drawn from the Revised Common Lectionary should you wish to pray along with the church calendar year, beginning with Week 1 in the season of Advent. See the lectionary guide on pages 315-316 to see which weeks correspond with the seasons of the church year.

Practicing Spiritual Reading As you read the essay or quotations, do so to hear the voice of God rather than to get information or seek an idea. Ask what God is saying to you through your reading. (Job, *A Guide to Retreat*, 15). Each week's Spiritual Reading section has two components.

The first is a brief essay written by Rueben P. Job. You may think of your own life experiences and how they enlighten your understanding of the theme of the week, the Scripture passage of the day, or the essay of the week.

Following the essay, there is a selection of quotations that have been chosen from a wide variety of sources to further illuminate the theme of the week and to prepare you for further spiritual reading from resources listed in the bibliography (pages 307-313).

Taking Time to Reflect is designed for you to pause and examine what you have heard and ask how it applies to your life situation. You may choose to meditate on Scripture, on one of the readings, or on your own life experience and ask what God is saying to you through this book and this time of reflection.

Making Our Requests Known is when you focus your prayers more precisely on specific things, persons, or events. The prayer that Jesus taught us is the model structure for our own prayer life. However, the structure of your prayers or your prayer time is determined more by your relationship to God and your particular needs at the moment than to any imposed structure. At a time of great thanksgiving, joy, pain, grief, question, fulfillment, loneliness, fear, confidence, or faith the state of our mind, heart, body, and spirit will dictate the form and content of your prayers and oftentimes the structure of your prayers as well.

Thanking God for Our Prayers and Life is the time, through either a closing prayer or Scripture passage, to offer your life, all you have, are, and hope to become, to God—and to invite God to do with you what is best with the full confidence that the God who loves you without limit will provide for you and invest your life in the work of God in good and meaningful ways.

Prayer at the End of the Day is a daily prayer practice to be offered at the end of each day in which you reflect upon the past day's experiences. At this time, as these prayers draw to a close, place all matters of the day—positive and negative—into God's hands and entrust them to God before you lie down to sleep.

Jesus was not a stranger to the needs and power of prayer. Some of his prayers are recorded in the Gospels and often he sought times of prayer and solitude. The sixth chapter of Mark reports that Jesus and the disciples were so busy they did not even have time to eat. Sound like anything you experience? Well, it was then that Jesus suggested, "Come by yourselves to a secluded place and rest for a while" (Mark 6:31). But when they got to the deserted place, the crowds were already there and Jesus saw them as sheep without a shepherd, had compassion on them, began to teach them, and when it grew late instructed the disciples to feed them (verses 33-34). The compassion of Jesus for the crowds is good news to us.

We do not embark on our life of prayer on our own. Whether we have been growing in our life with God and our pattern of prayer for decades or if we are just beginning, Jesus, who had compassion on the crowds in the deserted places of their lives, today has compassion on you and on me. And today we claim as our own his promise to the first disciples, "The Companion, the Holy Spirit, whom the Father will send in my name, will teach you everything and will remind you of everything I told you" (John 14:26).

And so we offer ourselves into the hands of God, ready to be taught, led, formed, and transformed as we daily turn our lives more fully toward God and listen and respond as we are taught and nurtured by the Holy Spirit. May the use of these practices for prayerful living bring new joy, peace, assurance, direction, awareness of God's presence with you, and fulfillment to your life as a follower of Jesus who teaches us how to pray. What more could we ask?

Weekly Readings and Themes

Week 1

Looking Forward

Approaching God with Intention

Holy God
of unconditional love
and unlimited presence,
I come to make myself fully available
to you, your will, and your way.

 Sit in silence and stillness for a few moments, lengthening the time each day as you are able.

Becoming Aware of God's Presence

Tell me all about your faithful love come morning time,
   because I trust you. (Psalm 143:8a)

Inviting God's Intervention

Show me the way I should go,
   because I offer my life up to you. (Psalm 143:8b)

Listening for God's Voice

Open yourself to hear what God is saying to you through the Scriptures.

This is what Isaiah, Amoz's son, saw concerning Judah and Jerusalem.

> In the days to come
> > the mountain of the LORD's house
> > will be the highest of the mountains.
> > It will be lifted above the hills;
> > > peoples will stream to it.
> Many nations will go and say,
> "Come, let's go up to the LORD's mountain,
> > to the house of Jacob's God
> > > so that he may teach us his ways
> > > and we may walk in God's paths."
> Instruction will come from Zion;
> > the LORD's word from Jerusalem.
> God will judge between the nations,
> > and settle disputes of mighty nations.
> Then they will beat their swords into
> iron plows
> > and their spears into pruning tools.
> Nation will not take up sword against nation;
> > they will no longer learn how to
> > make war.
>
> Come, house of Jacob,
> > let's walk by the LORD's light.
> > > (Isaiah 2:1-5)

Alternative Readings

Luke 21:25-36

Psalm 80:1-7, 17-19

1 Corinthians 1:3-9

Isaiah 1:10-20

1 Thessalonians 1:1-10

Luke 21:5-19

Practicing Spiritual Reading

As you read the essay and one or more quotations each day, do so with an openness for further contemplation on the week's theme. Ask God, Is there a word or prayer for my life in these words?

Ineffable moments are rare for most of us. The testimony of the saints confirms our own experience. While our hunger for God is universal and has been identified from the time of Adam and Eve to be our own, those peak moments of communion or union with God are extremely rare. They are there, perhaps to lure us or to reassure us, but they are not there on command or with predictable regularity. For the saints who have gone before and for us, much of life is lived out on the level plains. The plains of daily existence may be marked with deep awareness on the presence of One who is near and who sustains us, or the quiet companionship of One who guides and upholds, but there is awareness of a relationship that is life-giving. (Job, *A Guide to Retreat*, 19.)

 Perhaps the most startling thought that can inhabit the human imagination is that a man or a woman, earthbound and stuttering, can speak meaningfully of God. (Ben Campbell Johnson, *GodSpeech: Putting Divine Disclosures into Human Words*, 30.)

Today the heart of God is an open wound of love. He aches over our distance and preoccupation. He mourns that we do not draw near to him. He grieves that we have forgotten him. He weeps over our obsession with muchness and manyness. He longs for our presence. (Richard J. Foster, *Prayer: Finding the Heart's True Home*, 1.)

In prayer we say who in fact we are—not who we should be, nor who we wish we were, but who we are. All prayer begins with this confession. (Ann and Barry Ulanov, *Primary Speech: A Psychology of Prayer*, 1.)

We are like children being taught a job by a loving parent who teaches by allowing us to help with the job. And what is such guidance to a child by a loving parent worth unless there is an eager, but docile, response on the part of the child? The whole value of an interior life depends on this: that no bit of it ever is done alone because we think we know how, but always in response to the gentle guidance and teaching of God. (Evelyn Underhill, *The Ways of the Spirit*, 179.)

Living in the presence of and in harmony with the living God who is made known to us in Jesus Christ and companions us in the Holy Spirit is to live life from the inside out. It is to find our moral direction, our wisdom, our courage, our strength to live faithfully from the One who authored us. (Rueben P. Job, *Three Simple Rules: A Wesleyan Way of Living*, 54.)

Taking Time to Reflect

 Pause and recall what you have read and heard, as well as your own life experiences. Take note of anything that particularly catches your attention—perhaps a word, phrase, or image.

Making Our Requests Known

Focus your prayers more specifically on particular things, persons, or circumstances. The following petitions offer guidance:

Prayers for God's Creation and Our World
Prayers for All God's People
Prayers for the Church and All Who Seek God
Prayers for Our Neighbors
Prayers for Our Families and Friends
Prayers for Ourselves

Thanking God for Our Prayers and Life

Loving God,
Remind me often today where I find my identity.
May I never forget that I am your beloved child.
May I listen for and hear your faintest whisper,
Feel your slightest touch,
Respond quickly to your call,
Yield to your word of correction,
Rejoice in your companionship,
And serve you faithfully all the days of my life.

Thank you for hearing my prayers
And accepting my life.
I offer them to you as completely as I can
In the Name and Spirit of Jesus Christ. Amen.

Prayer at the End of the Day

Inviting God's Activity

Tender Shepherd of my soul, make yourself and your way known to me in this evening time of prayer and reflection. By the power of your presence, bring me to the end of the day whole, complete, and at peace with you, my neighbor, and myself. Grant a night of peaceful rest and send me forth tomorrow as a witness to your love and grace.

A Continuing Request

Create a clean heart for me, God;
> put a new, faithful spirit deep inside me! (Psalm 51:10)

Gathering the Day

Remembering—Reflect on the day's experiences.

Confessing—Own up to your own weakness, failure, and sin.

Forgiving—Ask for and accept God's forgiveness, and forgive yourself and all who may have injured you or those you love.

Thanksgiving—Give thanks for the gifts that God has granted this day.

Offering

My whole being clings to you;
> your strong hand upholds me. (Psalm 63:8)

Blessing

I will lie down and fall asleep in peace
> because you alone, Lord, let me live in safety. (Psalm 4:8)

Week 2

Where Righteousness Is at Home

Approaching God with Intention

I cry out to you because you answer me.
    So tilt your ears toward me now—
    listen to what I'm saying!
Manifest your faithful love in amazing ways
    because you are the one
    who saves those who take refuge in you,
    saving them from their attackers
    by your strong hand.
Watch me with the very pupil of your eye!
    Hide me in the protection of your wings. (Psalm 17:6-8)

 Sit in silence and stillness for a few moments, lengthening the time each day as you are able.

Becoming Aware of God's Presence

But according to his promise we are waiting for a new heaven and a new earth, where righteousness is at home.

(2 Peter 3:13)

Inviting God's Intervention

Happy are people who are hungry and thirsty for righteousness, because they will be fed until they are full. (Matthew 5:6)

Listening for God's Voice

Open yourself to hear what God is saying to you through the Scriptures.

Mary said,

"With all my heart I glorify the Lord!
    In the depths of who I am I rejoice in God my savior.
He has looked with favor on the low status of his servant.
        Look! From now on, everyone will consider me highly
        favored
            because the mighty one has done great things for me.
Holy is his name.
        He shows mercy to everyone,
            from one generation to the next,
            who honors him as God.
He has shown strength with his arm.
        He has scattered those with arrogant thoughts and proud
        inclinations.
        He has pulled the powerful down from their thrones
            and lifted up the lowly.
He has filled the hungry with good things
        and sent the rich away empty-handed.
He has come to the aid of his servant Israel,
            remembering his mercy,
        just as he promised to our ancestors,
            to Abraham and to Abraham's
            descendants forever." (Luke 1:46-55)

Alternative Readings

Isaiah 61:8-11
Psalm 85:1-2, 8-13
2 Corinthians 5:16-21
Psalm 1
James 3:13-18
Ephesians 4:17-24

Practicing Spiritual Reading

As you read the essay and one or more quotations each day, do so with an openness for further contemplation on the week's theme. Ask God, Is there a word or prayer for my life in these words?

We long for a world where righteousness is at home. It is a world envisioned by the prophets and saints of every age. It is a vision that is reflected in Mary's song and is still on the lips of the faithful everywhere. We yearn for a world where justice, fairness, equality, goodness, integrity, and well-doing are modeled in industry, government, school, home, and individual life. Deep in our hearts we know that it is a way of living that will result in a deep sense of well-being and peace for everyone. However, much as we would like to, most of us do not have the wisdom or power to transform the world. But we do have the wisdom and power to permit God to transform us. In our lives, and now and then in the world where we live, righteousness will be at home. You and I can become those persons who carry these gifts of grace to the world.

God's love is *the* foundation of our life. Upon it rests our ultimate identity, our integrity, our hope. It is the good news that sets us free. (Max Olivia, *Free to Pray, Free to Love: Growing in Prayer and Compassion*, 13.)

Before anything else, above all else, beyond everything else, God loves us. God loves us extravagantly, ridiculously, without limit or condition. God is in love with us; God is besotted with us. God yearns for us. (Roberta C. Bondi, *In Ordinary Time: Healing the Wounds of the Heart*, 22.)

Prayer is God's greatest provision for our spiritual life. Our relationship with God is impossible without prayer. We cannot know God's mind or heart without prayer. We cannot receive God's direction, hear God's voice, or respond to God's call without prayer. Since this is true, prayer is also God's greatest provision for all of life. It is the supreme means of grace given to all humankind. (Rueben P. Job, *A Wesleyan Spiritual Reader*, 16.)

Contemplative prayer is the world in which God can do anything. To move into that realm is the greatest adventure. It is to be open to the Infinite and hence to infinite possibilities. Our private, self-made worlds come to an end; a new world appears within and around us and the impossible becomes an everyday experience. (Thomas Keating, *Open Mind, Open Heart: The Contemplative Dimension of the Gospel*, 11.)

Taking Time to Reflect

 Pause and recall what you have read and heard, as well as your own life experiences. Take note of anything that particularly catches your attention—perhaps a word, phrase, or image.

Making Our Requests Known

Focus your prayers more specifically on particular things, persons, or circumstances. The following petitions offer guidance:

Prayers for God's Creation and Our World
Prayers for All God's People
Prayers for the Church and All Who Seek God
Prayers for Our Neighbors
Prayers for Our Families and Friends
Prayers for Ourselves

Thanking God for Our Prayers and Life

Creator God,
By the power of your grace,
transform us more and more
until we become beautiful reflections
of your presence and likeness
in all that we do and are,
as we offer all that we are and have
to you in the name and spirit of Christ.
Amen.

Prayer at the End of the Day

Inviting God's Activity

Tender Shepherd of my soul, make yourself and your way known to me in this evening time of prayer and reflection. By the power of your presence, bring me to the end of the day whole, complete, and at peace with you, my neighbor, and myself. Grant a night of peaceful rest and send me forth tomorrow as a witness to your love and grace.

A Continuing Request

Create a clean heart for me, God;
   put a new, faithful spirit deep inside me! (Psalm 51:10)

Gathering the Day

Remembering—Reflect on the day's experiences.

Confessing—Own up to your own weakness, failure, and sin.

Forgiving—Ask for and accept God's forgiveness, and forgive yourself and all who may have injured you or those you love.

Thanksgiving—Give thanks for the gifts that God has granted this day.

Offering

My whole being clings to you;
   your strong hand upholds me. (Psalm 63:8)

Blessing

I will lie down and fall asleep in peace
   because you alone, LORD, let me live in safety. (Psalm 4:8)

Week 3

Who Are You Looking For?

Approaching God with Intention

Loving God,
Come to me now and
Make yourself known to me
As I seek to quiet the noise of the world,
The anxiety of my heart and mind,
And the call of unfinished tasks
So that I might recognize
And welcome your voice.

 Sit in silence and stillness for a few moments, lengthening the time each day as you are able.

Becoming Aware of God's Presence

> Healthy people don't need a doctor, but sick people do. I didn't come to call righteous people but sinners to change their hearts and lives. (Luke 5:31-32)

Inviting God's Intervention

> Afterward, Jesus went out and saw a tax collector named Levi sitting at a kiosk for collecting taxes. Jesus said to him, "Follow me." (Luke 5:27)

Listening for God's Voice

Open yourself to hear what God is saying to you through the Scriptures.

> Now when John heard in prison about the things the Christ was doing, he sent word by his disciples to Jesus, asking, "Are you the one who is to come, or should we look for another?"
>
> Jesus responded, "Go, report to John what you hear and see. *Those who were blind are able to see.* Those who were crippled are walking. People with skin diseases are cleansed. Those *who were deaf now hear. Those who were dead are raised up. The poor have good news proclaimed to them.* Happy are those who don't stumble and fall because of me."
>
> When John's disciples had gone, Jesus spoke to the crowds about John: "What did you go out to the wilderness to see? A stalk blowing in the wind? What did you go out to see? A man dressed up in refined clothes? Look, those who wear refined clothes are in royal palaces. What did you go out to see? A prophet? Yes, I tell you, and more than a prophet. He is the one of whom it is written: *Look, I'm sending my messenger before you, who will prepare your way before you.*
>
> "I assure you that no one who has ever been born is greater than John the Baptist. Yet whoever is least in the kingdom of heaven is greater than he." (Matthew 11:2-11)

Alternative Readings

Isaiah 35:1-10
1 Thessalonians 5:16-24
Hebrews 12:1-2
Isaiah 56:1-8
Matthew 2:1-6
John 1:6-8, 19-28

Practicing Spiritual Reading

As you read the essay and one or more quotations each day, do so with an openness for further contemplation on the week's theme. Ask God, Is there a word or prayer for my life in these words?

Despite our tendency sometimes to follow lesser gods, we know that, as Christians, the God we profess is a particular God. We know that the call of Jesus to follow him is a call to follow the God he lovingly called *Abba* and to whom he fully gave his own life.

It is in Jesus that we have the clearest picture of who God is, what God does, and how God invites us to live as God's children. . . .

The God whom Jesus reveals shatters all of our little ideas about God and reveals a God who is author and creator of all there is. In Jesus we see a God who reverses the values of our culture and turns upside down our scheme of priorities, leaving us gasping at the sight of such bone-deep love, justice, and mercy. . . .

In Jesus we see a God who is never under our control but always free of any control, and who may act and create as it seems wise and is in keeping with God's will.

Jesus reveals a God who is always and forever beyond us, completely other than who we are, and yet who wants to come and dwell within us (John 14:23). Jesus reveals a God of love. (Rueben P. Job, *Three Simple Questions: Knowing the God of Love, Hope, and Purpose*, 19-22.)

 To pray is to change. This is a great grace. How good of God to provide a path whereby our lives can be taken over by love and joy and peace and patience and kindness and goodness and faithfulness and gentleness and self-control.

The movement inward comes first because without interior transformation the movement up into God's glory would overwhelm us and the movement out into ministry would destroy us. (Foster, *Prayer*, 6.)

Jesus teaches us that prayer is fundamentally a loving listening to God as he continually communicates his love to us at each movement. We pray when we are attentive to the presence of God. (George A. Maloney, *In Jesus We Trust*, 36-37.)

In his inaugural speech in the Gospel of Mark, Jesus tells the people that God's kingdom is among them, and then he calls them to *metanoia*, to a radical change of mind, body, heart, and soul. What he is saying is this: God's love is now available unconditionally and without restriction, but you must change your whole life if you are to receive it. (Robert Barron, *The Strangest Way: Walking the Christian Path*, 33.)

To be a follower of Jesus is to be a pilgrim, and it is to be on a journey that always leads us toward God's goodness. The Scriptures remind us that God loves us and seeks to sustain us in all of life. Therefore we can ask for guidance in the confidence that God's way, the very best way, will be made known to us. The vision of the promised land comes from God. The direction and strength to get there also come from God. But if we are to see the vision and to make the journey, we must be willing to give up what we have for that which is not yet fully realized. (Rueben P. Job, *A Guide to Spiritual Discernment*, 16.)

Taking Time to Reflect

 Pause and recall what you have read and heard, as well as your own life experiences. Take note of anything that particularly catches your attention—perhaps a word, phrase, or image.

Making Our Requests Known

Focus your prayers more specifically on particular things, persons, or circumstances. The following petitions offer guidance:

Prayers for God's Creation and Our World
Prayers for All God's People
Prayers for the Church and All Who Seek God
Prayers for Our Neighbors
Prayers for Our Families and Friends
Prayers for Ourselves

Thanking God for Our Prayers and Life

I give thanks to you with all my heart, LORD.
    I sing your praise before all other gods.
I bow toward your holy temple
    and thank your name
    for your loyal love and faithfulness
        because you have made your name and word
        greater than everything else.
On the day I cried out, you answered me.
    You encouraged me with inner strength. (Psalm 138:1-3)

Prayer at the End of the Day

Inviting God's Activity

Tender Shepherd of my soul, make yourself and your way known to me in this evening time of prayer and reflection. By the power of your presence, bring me to the end of the day whole, complete, and at peace with you, my neighbor, and myself. Grant a night of peaceful rest and send me forth tomorrow as a witness to your love and grace.

A Continuing Request

Create a clean heart for me, God;
    put a new, faithful spirit deep inside me! (Psalm 51:10)

Gathering the Day

Remembering—Reflect on the day's experiences.

Confessing—Own up to your own weakness, failure, and sin.

Forgiving—Ask for and accept God's forgiveness, and forgive yourself and all who may have injured you or those you love.

Thanksgiving—Give thanks for the gifts that God has granted this day.

Offering

My whole being clings to you;
    your strong hand upholds me. (Psalm 63:8)

Blessing

I will lie down and fall asleep in peace
    because you alone, LORD, let me live in safety. (Psalm 4:8)

Week 4

Here I Am

Approaching God with Intention

Creator God, author of all that is
and lover of all that you have made,
deepen our awareness of your mighty acts
past and present and your constant presence
with us every moment of our existence.
Invade our minds, senses, and hearts
like a quiet sunrise, a refreshing rain,
a beautiful bouquet, a commanding voice,
a trusted companion, and a loving touch—
because we want to know you
and remember who you are
with every breath we take. Amen.

 *Sit in silence and stillness for a few moments, lengthening the time
each day as you are able.*

Becoming Aware of God's Presence

Rejoice, favored one! The Lord is with you! (Luke 1:28)

Inviting God's Intervention

I am the Lord's servant. Let it be with me just as you have said.

(Luke 1:38)

Listening for God's Voice

Open yourself to hear what God is saying to you through the Scriptures.

In the year of King Uzziah's death, I saw the Lord sitting on a high and exalted throne, the edges of his robe filling the temple. Winged creatures were stationed around him. Each had six wings: with two they veiled their faces, with two their feet, and with two they flew about. They shouted to each other, saying:

"Holy, holy, holy is the LORD of heavenly forces! All the earth is filled with God's glory!"

The doorframe shook at the sound of their shouting, and the house was filled with smoke.

I said, "Mourn for me; I'm ruined! I'm a man with unclean lips, and I live among a people with unclean lips. Yet I've seen the king, the LORD of heavenly forces!"

Then one of the winged creatures flew to me, holding a glowing coal that he had taken from the altar with tongs. He touched my mouth and said, "See, this has touched your lips. Your guilt has departed, and your sin is removed."

Then I heard the Lord's voice saying, "Whom should I send, and who will go for us?"

I said, "I'm here; send me." (Isaiah 6:1-8)

Alternative Readings

Luke 1:26-38
Jeremiah 1:4-9
1 Samuel 3:1-10
Colossians 3:1-10
Micah 5:2-5a
Acts 9:10-19

Practicing Spiritual Reading

As you read the essay and one or more quotations each day, do so with an openness for further contemplation on the week's theme. Ask God, Is there a word or prayer for my life in these words?

To say that I am a Christian is really quite simple, but to live as a faithful follower of Jesus is another matter. Taking seriously the message of Jesus can be frightening and foreboding, because in my honest moments I know that on my own I cannot live the way of love that Jesus taught and lived. When I look at the immediate consequences of his life, I realize that the way of love is asking too much, and I am simply not up to living that way. . . .

Then, like a fresh burst of wind, the realization breaks in upon me: I am not asked to do this on my own! I am asked to follow Jesus, and that means not only to do and be what Jesus calls me to do and be, but also to accept the power and presence of God to make me more than I am and enable me to live as a beloved child of God. (Job, *Three Simple Rules*, 64-65.)

 Joy does not come from positive predictions about the state of the world. It does not depend on the ups and downs of the circumstances of our lives. Joy is based on spiritual knowledge that, while the world in which we live is shrouded in darkness, God has overcome the world. Jesus says it loudly and clearly: "In the world you will have troubles, but rejoice I have overcome the world."

The surprise is not that, unexpectedly, things turn out better than expected. No, the real surprise is that God's light is more real than all the darkness, that God's truth is more powerful than all human lies, that God's love is stronger than death. (Henri J. M. Nouwen, *Here and Now: Living in the Spirit*, 36-37.)

It is the quiet prayerful space of the early morning that enables us to be better attuned to God's particular call for us each day. Without such an intentional space for prayer, hearing the "voice" of God becomes quite difficult. (Robert J. Wicks, *Touching the Holy: Ordinariness, Self-Esteem, and Friendship*, 163.)

Let Jesus use you without consulting you. We let Him take what He wants from us. So take whatever He gives and give whatever He takes with a big smile. Accept the gifts of God and be deeply grateful. If He has given you great wealth, make use of it, try to share it with others, with those who don't have anything. Always share with others because even with a little help you may save them from becoming distressed. And don't take more than you need, that's all. Just accept whatever comes. (Mother Teresa, *A Simple Path*, 45.)

Taking Time to Reflect

 Pause and recall what you have read and heard, as well as your own life experiences. Take note of anything that particularly catches your attention—perhaps a word, phrase, or image.

Making Our Requests Known

Focus your prayers more specifically on particular things, persons, or circumstances. The following petitions offer guidance:

Prayers for God's Creation and Our World
Prayers for All God's People
Prayers for the Church and All Who Seek God
Prayers for Our Neighbors
Prayers for Our Families and Friends
Prayers for Ourselves

Thanking God for Our Prayers and Life

Sustaining God,
in whom we find our identity and our life,
thank you for this time apart with you.
I offer to you all of my life that I am able to give.
Accept and make holy
the gift of self I bring
and send me from this place
renewed, refreshed, and redirected
for effective ministry
in your name. Amen.

Prayer at the End of the Day

Inviting God's Activity

Tender Shepherd of my soul, make yourself and your way known to me in this evening time of prayer and reflection. By the power of your presence, bring me to the end of the day whole, complete, and at peace with you, my neighbor, and myself. Grant a night of peaceful rest and send me forth tomorrow as a witness to your love and grace.

A Continuing Request

Create a clean heart for me, God;
    put a new, faithful spirit deep inside me! (Psalm 51:10)

Gathering the Day

Remembering—Reflect on the day's experiences.

Confessing—Own up to your own weakness, failure, and sin.

Forgiving—Ask for and accept God's forgiveness, and forgive yourself and all who may have injured you or those you love.

Thanksgiving—Give thanks for the gifts that God has granted this day.

Offering

My whole being clings to you;
    your strong hand upholds me. (Psalm 63:8)

Blessing

I will lie down and fall asleep in peace
    because you alone, LORD, let me live in safety. (Psalm 4:8)

Week 5

Alarming Threats and Faithful Response

Approaching God with Intention

> Answer me when I cry out, my righteous God!
>> Set me free from my troubles!
>>> Have mercy on me!
>>> Listen to my prayer! (Psalm 4:1)

 Sit in silence and stillness for a few moments, lengthening the time each day as you are able.

Becoming Aware of God's Presence

> Open the gates of righteousness for me
>> so I can come in and give thanks to the LORD!
> This is the LORD's gate;
>> those who are righteous enter through it. (Psalm 118:19-20)

Inviting God's Intervention

> LORD, hear my prayer!
>> Let my cry reach you!
> Don't hide your face from me
>> in my time of trouble!
> Listen to me!
>> Answer me quickly as I cry out! (Psalm 102:1-2)

Listening for God's Voice

Open yourself to hear what God is saying to you through the Scriptures.

When Herod knew the magi had fooled him, he grew very angry. He sent soldiers to kill all the children in Bethlehem and in all the surrounding territory who were two years old and younger, according to the time that he had learned from the magi. This fulfilled the word spoken through Jeremiah the prophet:

A voice was heard in Ramah,
  weeping and much grieving.
    Rachel weeping for her children,
      and she did not want to be comforted,
        because they were no more.

After King Herod died, an angel from the Lord appeared in a dream to Joseph in Egypt. "Get up," the angel said, "and take the child and his mother and go to the land of Israel. Those who were trying to kill the child are dead." Joseph got up, took the child and his mother, and went to the land of Israel. But when he heard that Archelaus ruled over Judea in place of his father Herod, Joseph was afraid to go there. Having been warned in a dream, he went to the area of Galilee. He settled in a city called Nazareth so that what was spoken through the prophets might be fulfilled: He will be called a Nazarene. (Matthew 2:16-23)

Alternative Readings

Isaiah 12
Matthew 2:13-23
Psalm 148
John 7:37-39
Acts 10:34-43
2 Thessalonians 1:1-4

Practicing Spiritual Reading

As you read the essay and one or more quotations each day, do so with an openness for further contemplation on the week's theme. Ask God, Is there a word or prayer for my life in these words?

Our first child was born while we were living in a Chicago suburb. She was healthy, strong, and a delight as we watched her grow and develop. And then suddenly at nine months of age she developed a lung infection that the usual antibiotic could not overcome. Our doctor and pastor were with us when we were told she had a fifty/fifty chance of survival and our only hope was to take a specimen to a Chicago lab to see if an antibiotic could be found that would overcome the infection. With hearts filled with uncertainty and fear we agreed that regardless of the cost the specimen should be taken to the lab. The good news is that in a matter of hours the report came back that there was an antibiotic that could overcome the infection, and a short time later it was delivered to the hospital and given to our daughter.

When a child is threatened we immediately want to act to protect and save the child at all costs. The decision that Joseph and Mary made to follow the guidance of God's messenger meant great hardship but it also meant sparing the life of the child.

What are the threats that you feel for yourself, those you love, the children of the world? What is a faithful response in each situation? We do not know in advance, but we do know the One who can guide us to faithful response no matter the nature or size of the threat.

 Discernment at its best is the consequence of a daily and lifetime walk with God. A lifetime of such companionship produces profound results that range from guidance in decision making to transformation of one's life. Living a life of discernment, then, is a simple process of staying attentive to and open to God in all of the active and contemplative times of our lives. (Job, *A Guide to Spiritual Discernment*, 82.)

There is probably no one more truly radical than real persons of prayer because they are beholden to no ideology or economic system, but only to God. Both church and state are honestly threatened by true mystics. They can't be bought off because their rewards are elsewhere. (Richard Rohr, *Everything Belongs: The Gift of Contemplative Prayer*, 157.)

Saints are notoriously not interested in themselves, but passionately interested in God and other souls. (Underhill, *The Ways of the Spirit*, 91.)

Our culture says that ruthless competition is the key to success. Jesus says that ruthless compassion is the purpose of our journey. (Brennan Manning, *Ruthless Trust: The Ragamuffin's Path to God*, 169.)

We, like the apostle Paul, know the reality of our weakness. We often fail to do what we plan to do and often do that which we determine not to do. We need to remind each other that our salvation is in Jesus Christ and not in our works, good or otherwise. We are saved by grace, through faith in God, and not by our efforts, no matter how noble or extensive. (Job, *A Guide to Retreat*, 61–62.)

Taking Time to Reflect

 Pause and recall what you have read and heard, as well as your own life experiences. Take note of anything that particularly catches your attention—perhaps a word, phrase, or image.

Making Our Requests Known

Focus your prayers more specifically on particular things, persons, or circumstances. The following petitions offer guidance:

Prayers for God's Creation and Our World
Prayers for All God's People
Prayers for the Church and All Who Seek God
Prayers for Our Neighbors
Prayers for Our Families and Friends
Prayers for Ourselves

Thanking God for Our Prayers and Life

God,
Greater than anything I can imagine,
Holiness purer and more brilliant than light,
Mercy that forgives, redeems, and leads to righteousness,
Love that accepts and embraces me just as I am,
Grace that sustains and molds me into more than I am,
Promised presence that will never forsake or leave me alone,

I tremble in awe of such greatness and love;
I fall on my knees in gratitude and humility;
I yield my will to yours;
I declare that I am yours alone
    and invite you to do with me what you will
As I walk in the light and life
    of your unswerving presence.

Prayer at the End of the Day

Inviting God's Activity

Tender Shepherd of my soul, make yourself and your way known to me in this evening time of prayer and reflection. By the power of your presence, bring me to the end of the day whole, complete, and at peace with you, my neighbor, and myself. Grant a night of peaceful rest and send me forth tomorrow as a witness to your love and grace.

A Continuing Request

Create a clean heart for me, God;
  put a new, faithful spirit deep inside me! (Psalm 51:10)

Gathering the Day

Remembering—Reflect on the day's experiences.

Confessing—Own up to your own weakness, failure, and sin.

Forgiving—Ask for and accept God's forgiveness, and forgive yourself and all who may have injured you or those you love.

Thanksgiving—Give thanks for the gifts that God has granted this day.

Offering

My whole being clings to you;
  your strong hand upholds me. (Psalm 63:8)

Blessing

I will lie down and fall asleep in peace
  because you alone, Lord, let me live in safety. (Psalm 4:8)

Week 6

Waiting for the Light

Approaching God with Intention

Creator of all that exists
    and lover of all you have made,
Bless me with eyes to see your presence
    in the world you love,
    ears to hear your tender voice of guidance,
    and courage to say,
"Here I am, use me this day
    for I am yours."

 Sit in silence and stillness for a few moments, lengthening the time each day as you are able.

Becoming Aware of God's Presence

> My presence will go with you, and I will give you rest.
> (Exodus 33:14a NRSV)

Inviting God's Intervention

> Now if I have found favor in your sight, show me your ways, so that I may know you and find favor in your sight.
> (Exodus 33:13 NRSV)

Listening for God's Voice

Open yourself to hear what God is saying to you through the Scriptures.

Alternative Readings

Isaiah 60:1-6

Matthew 2:1-2

Psalm 119:97-105

1 Peter 2:9-10

Acts 26:19-23

Genesis 1:1-8

In the beginning was the Word
  and the Word was with God
  and the Word was God.
The Word was with God in the beginning.
Everything came into being through the Word,
  and without the Word
  nothing came into being.
What came into being
  through the Word was life,
  and the life was the light for all people.
The light shines in the darkness,
  and the darkness doesn't extinguish the light. (John 1:1-5)

Practicing Spiritual Reading

As you read the essay and one or more quotations each day, do so with an openness for further contemplation on the week's theme. Ask God, Is there a word or prayer for my life in these words?

The gift of a robust and vibrant faith is not given easily or often. We may not experience the dark night of the soul that St. John of the Cross experienced, endured, and with which he wrestled until he found some joy and peace as the darkness yielded truth and light. But most of us at some point in our lives experience a sense of abandonment, unworthiness, aloneness that is as palpable in its sorrow as we want the presence of God to be joyful for us. Epiphany assures us that the light is coming, and the darkness of confusion, illness, sinfulness, doubt, and violence that grip our world and darken our world will not last. As Martin Luther King Jr. said in the darkest days of the struggle for racial justice, "Darkness cannot drive out darkness: only light can do that" (Martin Luther King Jr., *A Testament of Hope: The Essential Writings of Martin Luther King Jr.*, 594). So we wait, we endure, we watch, we pray, and we trust that one day the light will come and the darkness will be no more.

A new beginning! We must learn to live each day, each hour, yes, each minute as a new beginning, as a unique opportunity to make everything new. Imagine that we could live each moment as a moment pregnant with new life. Imagine that we could live each day as a day full of promises. Imagine that we could walk through the new year always listening to a voice saying to us: "I have a gift for you and can't wait for you to see it!" (Nouwen, *Here and Now*, 16.)

So according to the New Testament, the dream of a liberator, and the dream of peace, is not merely a dream. The liberator is already present and his power already among us. We can follow him, even today making visible something of the peace, liberty, and righteousness of the kingdom that he will complete. It is no longer impossible. It has become possible for us in fellowship with him. Let us share in his new creation of the world and—born again to a living hope—live as new men and women. (Jürgen Moltmann, "The Disarming Child," in *Watch for the Light: Readings for Advent and Christmas*, 320.)

Let us keep staunch in our eagerness to do whatever comes to us of the truth. Then there will be knocks on our door, over and over, and God's coming will not be hidden. For devoted hearts the light will keep dawning from him who is merciful and compassionate. (Christoph Friedrich Blumhardt, "Action in Waiting," in *Watch for the Light: Readings for Advent and Christmas*, 12.)

After a while, secularism is boring. It's a dead-end vision; in a secular world, the universe is not enchanted. The bush doesn't burn; it's just a shrub. American culture wants to break out of secularism. Materialism doesn't name our reality adequately . . .

It's like the soul is saying, "There is something more." *The spiritual world is hidden and perfectly revealed in the physical world.* That is the Christ Icon. That's why Jesus is so important; he makes visible the hiding place of God. His body is the revelation of the essential mystery. The material world is the hiding place of God. (Rohr, *Everything Belongs*, 116.)

Taking Time to Reflect

 Pause and recall what you have read and heard, as well as your own life experiences. Take note of anything that particularly catches your attention—perhaps a word, phrase, or image.

Making Our Requests Known

Focus your prayers more specifically on particular things, persons, or circumstances. The following petitions offer guidance:

Prayers for God's Creation and Our World
Prayers for All God's People
Prayers for the Church and All Who Seek God
Prayers for Our Neighbors
Prayers for Our Families and Friends
Prayers for Ourselves

Thanking God for Our Prayers and Life

Loving God,
I offer open hands, open mind, open heart,
    and a willing spirit
    to hear continually your calling and sending voice.
I abandon my life into your care
    with the assurance that you will lead me
    in paths of righteousness and goodness. Amen.

Prayer at the End of the Day

Inviting God's Activity

Tender Shepherd of my soul, make yourself and your way known to me in this evening time of prayer and reflection. By the power of your presence, bring me to the end of the day whole, complete, and at peace with you, my neighbor, and myself. Grant a night of peaceful rest and send me forth tomorrow as a witness to your love and grace.

A Continuing Request

Create a clean heart for me, God;
>put a new, faithful spirit deep inside me! (Psalm 51:10)

Gathering the Day

Remembering—Reflect on the day's experiences.

Confessing—Own up to your own weakness, failure, and sin.

Forgiving—Ask for and accept God's forgiveness, and forgive yourself and all who may have injured you or those you love.

Thanksgiving—Give thanks for the gifts that God has granted this day.

Offering

My whole being clings to you;
>your strong hand upholds me. (Psalm 63:8)

Blessing

I will lie down and fall asleep in peace
>because you alone, LORD, let me live in safety. (Psalm 4:8)

When God
Gets Our Attention

Approaching God with Intention

Lord, you have examined me.
  You know me.
You know when I sit down and when I stand up.
  Even from far away, you comprehend my plans.
You study my traveling and resting.
  You are thoroughly familiar with all my ways.
There isn't a word on my tongue, Lord,
  that you don't already know completely.
You surround me—front and back.
  You put your hand on me.
That kind of knowledge is too much for me;
  it's so high above me that I can't fathom it. (Psalm 139:1-6)

Sit in silence and stillness for a few moments, lengthening the time each day as you are able.

Becoming Aware of God's Presence

One day at nearly three o'clock in the afternoon, he clearly saw an angel from God in a vision. The angel came to him and said, "Cornelius!" (Acts 10:3)

Inviting God's Intervention

While Peter was brooding over the vision, the Spirit interrupted him, "Look! Three people are looking for you. Go downstairs. Don't ask questions; just go with them because I have sent them."

(Acts 10:19-20)

Listening for God's Voice

Open yourself to hear what God is saying to you through the Scriptures.

Alternative Readings
John 1:29-34
Luke 8:19-21
John 1:43-51
Psalm 29
Mark 2:13-17
Mark 6:53-56

But here is my servant, the one I uphold;
    my chosen, who brings me delight.
I've put my spirit upon him;
    he will bring justice to the nations.
He won't cry out or shout aloud
    or make his voice heard in public.
He won't break a bruised reed;
    he won't extinguish a faint wick,
    but he will surely bring justice.
He won't be extinguished or broken
    until he has established justice in the land.
The coastlands await his teaching. . . .

I, the LORD, have called you for a good reason.
    I will grasp your hand and guard you,
    and give you as a covenant to the people,
    as a light to the nations,
    to open blind eyes, to lead the prisoners from prison,
    and those who sit in darkness from the dungeon.
I am the LORD;
    that is my name;
    I don't hand out my glory to others
        or my praise to idols.

The things announced in the past—look—they've already happened,
> but I'm declaring new things.
> Before they even appear,
> I tell you about them. (Isaiah 42:1-4, 6-9)

Practicing Spiritual Reading

As you read the essay and one or more quotations each day, do so with an openness for further contemplation on the week's theme. Ask God, Is there a word or prayer for my life in these words?

Like a sharp clap of thunder, God can get our attention. But at other times God gets our attention with something that may be more like a gentle breeze touching our cheek, or a simple thought or urge that will not let us go. At the baptism of Jesus, a voice from heaven got the attention of those gathered to see the event. However, it was not so much the voice from heaven but the message that got the attention of everyone. The Son of God, the Beloved, with whom God is well pleased, was a message that got everyone's attention. Our task is to listen and pay attention so that we do not miss the gentle whisper or that sharp clap of thunder. They often come unannounced and from many sources, such as Scripture, prayer, worship, events of the day, and other totally unexpected sources. God's presence, power, direction, love, and companionship are continually being revealed.

It is so very simple and so very complete. We like to make it complex, hard to understand, and easy to avoid. But Jesus had a way of cutting through all the rules and their explanations to reveal the core truth of a faithful life. . . . His teaching was so clear it was hard to miss the point and so profound that it would take a lifetime of practice to fulfill its challenge. (Job, *When You Pray* 2009, 214.)

Even if we are not paying attention to God, God is paying attention to us. Even when we think our faith is but a smoldering wick, God is still full of faith in us and continues the sweep of love and gracious divine presence no matter where we are or what we are about. (Rueben P. Job, *Life Stories*, 66.)

Prayer is an invitation to God to intervene in our lives, to let His will prevail in our affairs. (Abraham J. Heschel, *I Asked for Wonder: A Spiritual Anthology*, 28.)

One excellent method of maintaining inward calmness and freedom is to keep putting aside all useless reflections on the past, whether of regret or self-satisfaction. When one duty is accomplished, go steadily on with the next, confining your attention entirely to the one thing God gives you to do, and not putting off difficulties for the future any more than dwelling on regrets for the past. Again, accustom yourself to make frequent brief acts of God's presence through the day amid all your activities. Whenever you are conscious that anxiety or disturbance are springing up within, calm yourself in this way: Cut yourself off from all that is not of God. (François Fénelon, *The Royal Way of the Cross*, 127.)

Taking Time to Reflect

Pause and recall what you have read and heard, as well as your own life experiences. Take note of anything that particularly catches your attention—perhaps a word, phrase, or image.

Making Our Requests Known

Focus your prayers more specifically on particular things, persons, or circumstances. The following petitions offer guidance:

Prayers for God's Creation and Our World
Prayers for All God's People
Prayers for the Church and All Who Seek God
Prayers for Our Neighbors
Prayers for Our Families and Friends
Prayers for Ourselves

Thanking God for Our Prayers and Life

Grant to me, O God,
    the continual guidance, strength, and help
    of your Holy Spirit
    so that I may serve faithfully.
Defend and uphold me
    and grant me grace to live in such a way
    as to please you
    and reflect your presence to others.
Hear and accept my prayer
as I offer it and my life
to you in gratitude
for your steadfast love.
In the name of Christ. Amen.

Prayer at the End of the Day

Inviting God's Activity

Tender Shepherd of my soul, make yourself and your way known to me in this evening time of prayer and reflection. By the power of your presence, bring me to the end of the day whole, complete, and at peace with you, my neighbor, and myself. Grant a night of peaceful rest and send me forth tomorrow as a witness to your love and grace.

A Continuing Request

Create a clean heart for me, God;
>   put a new, faithful spirit deep inside me! (Psalm 51:10)

Gathering the Day

Remembering—Reflect on the day's experiences.

Confessing—Own up to your own weakness, failure, and sin.

Forgiving—Ask for and accept God's forgiveness, and forgive yourself and all who may have injured you or those you love.

Thanksgiving—Give thanks for the gifts that God has granted this day.

Offering

My whole being clings to you;
>   your strong hand upholds me. (Psalm 63:8)

Blessing

I will lie down and fall asleep in peace
>   because you alone, LORD, let me live in safety. (Psalm 4:8)

Prayer Practice

Attentiveness and Expectancy

A friend once told me about a period in his life when he was being awakened every morning at 3:00. Being a person of prayer, he began asking God for insight into this upsetting experience. The answer to his prayer came quickly and clearly. "This seems to be the only time I can get your attention." He accepted the answer and began a practice of prayer at 3:00 every morning. He discovered that his life of prayer grew intensely.

Paying attention to everything that is happening in your life and viewing circumstances, situations, and experiences through "spiritual eyes" can be a helpful prayer practice. Be alert for those moments when you sense God is seeking your attention each day. Give attention to what you discovered; then respond, expecting God to work in your life.

Sometime today or this week, practice attentiveness and expectancy, anticipating unexpected insights or realizations. Pay attention to connections between things you are reading, hearing, or seeing. By approaching prayer with attentiveness and expectancy, you will position yourself to receive from God. (Job, *Listen*, 102.)

Week 8

Come and See

Approaching God with Intention

Loving God,
Who understands before I form my prayer,
Who hears when I call and translates my humble words
    into beautiful hymns of gratitude and praise
And responds to my uncertain cry for help
    with assurance, peace, and palpable presence,

Here I am as fully in your presence
    as I am able to be,
Offering my fears, my needs, my hopes,
    my love, and my life,
For I am yours and belong to no other.

 Sit in silence and stillness for a few moments, lengthening the time each day as you are able.

Becoming Aware of God's Presence

> The LORD is close to everyone who calls out to him,
>   to all who call out to him sincerely. (Psalm 145:18)

Inviting God's Intervention

Let my cry reach you, LORD;
> help me understand according to what you've said.
>> (Psalm 119:169)

Listening for God's Voice

Open yourself to hear what God is saying to you through the Scriptures.

The next day Jesus wanted to go into Galilee, and he found Philip. Jesus said to him, "Follow me." Philip was from Bethsaida, the hometown of Andrew and Peter.

Philip found Nathanael and said to him, "We have found the one Moses wrote about in the Law and the Prophets: Jesus, Joseph's son, from Nazareth."

Nathanael responded, "Can anything from Nazareth be good?"

Philip said, "Come and see."

Jesus saw Nathanael coming toward him and said about him, "Here is a genuine Israelite in whom there is no deceit."

Nathanael asked him, "How do you know me?"

Jesus answered, "Before Philip called you, I saw you under the fig tree."

Nathanael replied, "Rabbi, you are God's Son. You are the king of Israel."

Jesus answered, "Do you believe because I told you that I saw you under the fig tree? You will see greater things than these! I assure you that you will see heaven open and God's angels going up to heaven and down to earth on the Human One."
(John 1:43-51)

Alternative Readings
1 Samuel 3:1-10
John 2:1-11
Luke 7:36-50
Acts 17:1-9
Isaiah 62:1-5
Matthew 12:15-21

Practicing Spiritual Reading

As you read the essay and one or more quotations each day, do so with an openness for further contemplation on the week's theme. Ask God, Is there a word or prayer for my life in these words?

Often our image and understanding of God is far too small. When Nathanael first heard of Jesus, he was skeptical about anything good coming out of Nazareth. Philip responded by inviting him to come and see Jesus for himself. Firsthand experience always trumps what others may say about God and most other things as well. The writer of Colossians says that Jesus is the "image of the invisible God, the firstborn of all creation; for in him all things in heaven and on earth were created . . ." (1:15-16 NRSV). The first disciples had little to go on but the word of a friend until they began to hang out with Jesus themselves. Then they discovered that Jesus was the real thing. He really was more than just a good man and finally they were able to identify him as Messiah and Son of God. This week we face a few honest questions that the disciples raised about who Jesus really was. Do we know who Jesus is? May we have the courage to face our own questions and to do as those early disciples did, give ourselves to living close enough to Jesus to really get to know who he is and who God is as he gives a clear picture of the relationship between his beloved Abba and himself.

The greatest gift I have ever received from Jesus Christ has been the Abba experience. "No one knows the Son except the Father, just as no one knows the Father except the Son and those to whom the Son chooses to reveal him" (Matthew 11:27, The Jerusalem Bible). My dignity as Abba's child is my most coherent sense of self. When I seek to fashion a self-image from the adulation of others and the inner voice whispers, *You've arrived; you're a player in the kingdom enterprise*, there is no truth in that self-concept. When I sink into despondency and the inner voice whispers, *You are a no good fraud, a hypocrite, and a dilettante*, there is no truth in any image shaped from that message. (Brennan Manning, *Abba's Child: The Cry of the Heart for Intimate Belonging*, 44-45.)

We are not left on our own to learn how to pray or how to discern God's will; our Companion, the Holy Spirit, is our teacher and guide as we learn how to live more fully in relationship with God. It is God who chooses to make our way known to us, and it is God who does the revealing, leading, and instructing. (Job, *Listen*, 12–13.)

A student of mine shared that he believed that all prayer begins with God. This was a totally new idea for me. I had always held the belief that prayer was up to me. I had to initiate the communication; I had to go to God; I had to get God's attention. Considering that God was the initiator of the prayer relationship turned everything upside down. God was already present. God was waiting for me to respond to God's invitation. All I had to do was say yes. (Jane E. Vennard, *A Praying Congregation: The Art of Teaching Spiritual Practice*, 37.)

True spiritual leaders must first become and then remain friends of God. As the apostle Paul wrote, "While we live, we are always being given up to death for Jesus' sake, so that the life of Jesus may be made visible in our mortal flesh" (2 Corinthians 4:11 NRSV). In other words, spiritual leaders become the visible presence of Jesus in the world. (Rueben P. Job, *Becoming a Praying Congregation: Churchwide Leadership Tools*, 8.)

Taking Time to Reflect

Pause and recall what you have read and heard, as well as your own life experiences. Take note of anything that particularly catches your attention—perhaps a word, phrase, or image.

Making Our Requests Known

Focus your prayers more specifically on particular things, persons, or circumstances. The following petitions offer guidance:

Prayers for God's Creation and Our World
Prayers for All God's People
Prayers for the Church and All Who Seek God
Prayers for Our Neighbors
Prayers for Our Families and Friends
Prayers for Ourselves

Thanking God for Our Prayers and Life

I will thank you, LORD, with all my heart;
    I will talk about all your wonderful acts.
I will celebrate and rejoice in you;
    I will sing praises to your name, Most High. . . .

Have mercy on me, LORD!
    Just look how I suffer
    because of those who hate me.
But you are the one who brings me back
        from the very gates of death
            so I can declare all your praises,
            so I can rejoice in your salvation
            in the gates of Daughter Zion. (Psalm 9:1-2, 13-14)

Prayer at the End of the Day

Inviting God's Activity

Tender Shepherd of my soul, make yourself and your way known to me in this evening time of prayer and reflection. By the power of your presence, bring me to the end of the day whole, complete, and at peace with you, my neighbor, and myself. Grant a night of peaceful rest and send me forth tomorrow as a witness to your love and grace.

A Continuing Request

> Create a clean heart for me, God;
>> put a new, faithful spirit deep inside me! (Psalm 51:10)

Gathering the Day

Remembering—Reflect on the day's experiences.

Confessing—Own up to your own weakness, failure, and sin.

Forgiving—Ask for and accept God's forgiveness, and forgive yourself and all who may have injured you or those you love.

Thanksgiving—Give thanks for the gifts that God has granted this day.

Offering

> My whole being clings to you;
>> your strong hand upholds me. (Psalm 63:8)

Blessing

> I will lie down and fall asleep in peace
>> because you alone, LORD, let me live in safety. (Psalm 4:8)

Week 9

Follow Me

Approaching God with Intention

> I take refuge in you, LORD.
> > Please never let me be put to shame.
> > > Rescue me by your righteousness!
> Listen closely to me!
> > Deliver me quickly;
> > > be a rock that protects me;
> > > be a strong fortress that saves me!
> You are definitely my rock and my fortress.
> > Guide me and lead me for the sake of your good name!
> > > (Psalm 31:1-3)

 Sit in silence and stillness for a few moments, lengthening the time each day as you are able.

Becoming Aware of God's Presence

> The LORD is a sun and shield;
> > God is favor and glory.
> The LORD gives—doesn't withhold!—good things
> > to those who walk with integrity.
> LORD of heavenly forces,
> > those who trust in you are truly happy! (Psalm 84:11-12)

Inviting God's Intervention

> Have mercy on me, God;
> > have mercy on me
> > because I have taken refuge in you.
> > I take refuge
> > in the shadow of your wings
> > > until destruction passes by. (Psalm 57:1)

Listening for God's Voice

Open yourself to hear what God is saying to you through the Scriptures.

> Now I encourage you, brothers and sisters, in the name of our Lord Jesus Christ: Agree with each other and don't be divided into rival groups. Instead, be restored with the same mind and the same purpose. My brothers and sisters, Chloe's people gave me some information about you, that you're fighting with each other. What I mean is this: that each one of you says, "I belong to Paul," "I belong to Apollos," "I belong to Cephas," "I belong to Christ." Has Christ been divided? Was Paul crucified for you, or were you baptized in Paul's name? Thank God that I didn't baptize any of you, except Crispus and Gaius, so that nobody can say that you were baptized in my name! Oh, I baptized the house of Stephanas too. Otherwise, I don't know if I baptized anyone else. Christ didn't send me to baptize but to preach the good news. And Christ didn't send me to preach the good news with clever words so that Christ's cross won't be emptied of its meaning.

> The message of the cross is foolishness to those who are being destroyed. But it is the power of God for those of us who are being saved.
> > (1 Corinthians 1:10-18)

Alternative Readings
Matthew 4:12-23
Isaiah 6:1-8
Luke 4:14-21
Psalm 27:1, 4-9
Mark 1:14-20
Jeremiah 1:4-10

Practicing Spiritual Reading

As you read the essay and one or more quotations each day, do so with an openness for further contemplation on the week's theme. Ask God, Is there a word or prayer for my life in these words?

To live in Christ is to give all that we are, have, and hope to become to God's gracious direction. This is to enter into "fellowship" with God in a new and nurturing way—a way that leads to assurance of salvation and life abundant and eternal. It is a way that leads to the confidence and comfort that only companionship with Jesus Christ can bring. And it is a way that leads to definite and decisive response on the part of the believer.

In a world where institutions and individuals seem to be unworthy of trust, the believer finds in God one who is completely trustworthy. Thus it is possible to offer one's life, without reservation, and as totally as we are able, to this trustworthy God. Because God can be trusted, we can give ourselves to God without fear or anxiety that we will be deceived or disappointed. This kind of trust leads more and more to the living out of our faith. Life in Christ not only brings assurance and hope, it also begins to show some of the characteristics of Christ within the life of the believer. It is to have the image of God within each of us restored and made visible to ourselves and to others.

We have often seen children take on the qualities of their parents and students begin to reflect in their lives the life and ways of their teachers. To live in an intimate relationship with Christ is to begin to act like Christ, to think like Christ, and to be Christ-like in all of our living. (Job, *A Wesleyan Spiritual Reader*, 36-37.)

The conviction ran deep that because of personal commitment and the power of God at work in a person's life, Christians were to be different. Their goals and priorities were not determined by the culture, or even the church, but by a daily companionship with Jesus Christ. The love of God and neighbor led them to stand against all that was destructive of humankind. The consistent stand against injustice and the untiring efforts to create laws and institutions that brought healing, help, and hope to all people set them apart, often to their peril and pain. . . .

The only thing that mattered was faithfulness to God. (Job, *A Wesleyan Spiritual Reader*, 193.)

I am inhabited, says Jesus in Luke 4:18, by a spirit, pervaded by it, so that the entirety of my life is evidence of this occupying spirit. To be possessed by a spirit is to be consumed, taken over. The spirit of our lives is our total self, who we really are. It is the self that is not confined to time and place. It is the self that spans all our experiences and responses. It is the self that is our truest being. Spirituality is the process that leads to true selfhood. If we are Christians, it is a movement into Christ's path. (Joan Puls, *Seek Treasures in Small Fields: Everyday Holiness*, 160.)

Maybe the real scariness of conversion lies in admitting that God can work in us however, whenever, and through whatever means God chooses. If the incarnation of Jesus Christ teaches us anything, it is that conversion is not one-size-fits-all. Christian conversion is, in fact, incarnational; it is worked out by each individual within the community of faith. I believe that this is what Paul means by asking Christians to conform themselves to Christ. (Kathleen Norris, *Amazing Grace: A Vocabulary of Faith*, 42.)

In following Jesus, we are shown the way that leads toward the Father. Our life is not aimless; it has a destination. We have not been left to wander in the desert; the Shepherd has come to seek what is lost and bring us home.

Jesus has gone before us. In the words of John 13:1, he has made the crossing from this world toward the Father and summons us to come after him. (Michael Casey, *Toward God: The Ancient Wisdom of Western Prayer*, 2.)

Taking Time to Reflect

Pause and recall what you have read and heard, as well as your own life experiences. Take note of anything that particularly catches your attention—perhaps a word, phrase, or image.

Making Our Requests Known

Focus your prayers more specifically on particular things, persons, or circumstances. The following petitions offer guidance:

Prayers for God's Creation and Our World
Prayers for All God's People
Prayers for the Church and All Who Seek God
Prayers for Our Neighbors
Prayers for Our Families and Friends
Prayers for Ourselves

Thanking God for Our Prayers and Life

Faithful Guide and Companion,
continue to speak to me
the words of guidance,
correction, encouragement
and love that I need.
And send me to meet this day
with your power
and presence
to go where Jesus Christ leads me
and live as your faithful disciple
all day long.

Prayer at the End of the Day

Inviting God's Activity

Tender Shepherd of my soul, make yourself and your way known to me in this evening time of prayer and reflection. By the power of your presence, bring me to the end of the day whole, complete, and at peace with you, my neighbor, and myself. Grant a night of peaceful rest and send me forth tomorrow as a witness to your love and grace.

A Continuing Request

Create a clean heart for me, God;
    put a new, faithful spirit deep inside me! (Psalm 51:10)

Gathering the Day

Remembering—Reflect on the day's experiences.

Confessing—Own up to your own weakness, failure, and sin.

Forgiving—Ask for and accept God's forgiveness, and forgive yourself and all who may have injured you or those you love.

Thanksgiving—Give thanks for the gifts that God has granted this day.

Offering

My whole being clings to you;
    your strong hand upholds me. (Psalm 63:8)

Blessing

I will lie down and fall asleep in peace
    because you alone, Lord, let me live in safety. (Psalm 4:8)

Week 10

Teach Us How to Live

Approaching God with Intention

Loving Teacher,
Help us to open our minds, hearts,
    and entire lives to you.
Come, speak to us,
Teach us,
Lead us,
    and form us
    until we are more and more like you
For we are yours.

 *Sit in silence and stillness for a few moments, lengthening the time
each day as you are able.*

Becoming Aware of God's Presence

Living in the Most High's shelter,
    camping in the Almighty's shade,
I say to the LORD, "You are my refuge, my stronghold!
    You are my God—the one I trust!" (Psalm 91:1-2)

Inviting God's Intervention

Teach me your way, LORD,
> so that I can walk in your truth.
> Make my heart focused
> only on honoring your name.
> I give thanks to you, my LORD, my God,
> with all my heart,
> and I will glorify your name forever. (Psalm 86:11-12)

Listening for God's Voice

Open yourself to hear what God is saying to you through the Scriptures.

Who can live in your tent, LORD?
> Who can dwell on your holy mountain?
> The person who
> lives free of blame,
> does what is right,
>   and speaks the truth sincerely;
> who does no damage with their talk,
> does no harm to a friend,
> doesn't insult a neighbor;
> someone who despises
>   those who act wickedly,
>   but who honors those
>   who honor the LORD;
> someone who keeps their promise even when it hurts;
> someone who doesn't lend money with interest,
> who won't accept a bribe against any innocent person.
> Whoever does these things will never stumble. (Psalm 15)

Alternative Readings

Mark 6:1-13
Luke 11:1-13
Acts 5:33-42
Matthew 23:1-12
Luke 12:1-12
Psalm 25:1-10

Practicing Spiritual Reading

As you read the essay and one or more quotations each day, do so with an openness for further contemplation on the week's theme. Ask God, Is there a word or prayer for my life in these words?

When the disciples asked Jesus to teach them how to pray, he taught them the prayer that has been our pattern of prayer ever since. In the Lord's Prayer, Jesus instructed them in prayer, but he did far more than teach the disciples how to pray. He taught them how to live. In Luke's record, Jesus reminds the disciples to stay focused, not on their need or on themselves, but on God. Our culture tells us in a thousand ways to stay focused on ourselves and outdo one another by caring for ourselves first. Jesus tells us that the best way to live fully and faithfully is to outdo one another in loving God and neighbor. To follow Jesus is to choose for ourselves the best way to live.

 In the garden of our souls we are both the farmer and the seed. We've been planted. Our awakening experience has happened. Staying awake is the problem. Our soil soon becomes crowded with weeds. . . . How can we tend the garden of our souls? . . . These monastics were people like you and me. They felt the same impulse we do—they needed help. To find that help, they went to visit the early hermits, quiet dwellers in the desert and asked them, "How do you do it?" "How can I do it?" These wise persons taught them to guard their hearts, to watch their thoughts, to spend time in vigils, to fast, to confess, to practice ceaseless prayer, to practice the prayer of the heart, and to do manual labor, to name a few of the recommended practices. (Mary Margaret Funk, *Tools Matter for Practicing the Spiritual Life*, 1.)

Read the Bible, pray personally and corporately, fast, worship, receive the sacrament, and I believe you will discover a multitude of resources entering your life through the disciplined use of the means of grace. While we cannot force God to love us, redeem us, or sustain us, we can, through the means of grace, place ourselves in a position to receive God's great and good gifts each day. (Job, *A Wesleyan Spiritual Reader*, 92.)

God's gifts have come through my imagination, as in the times I have suddenly discovered a new image that helps me speak about prayer; they have come through other people with their questions, experiences, and invitations that stretch me into areas of discomfort; and they have come through the love of family, friends, and community who have encouraged and sustained me as my ministry unfolded. . . . There are times when I begin a presentation, wondering how I ever got to this place. That doubt reminds me to breathe a prayer for guidance and to teach about the wonder and mystery of God as best I can. (Vennard, *A Praying Congregation*, 97.)

We as individuals are not always inspired or capable; we don't always believe what it is we know we are supposed to pray. The communal liturgies that hold old sacred prayers offer us a structure, a history, and a way of holding each other together through joyous times and heartbreaks. The prayers that we know in our hearts are the prayers that can carry us through our lives, and they are also the prayers that we can offer to carry others through. (Becca Stevens, "Give Us This Day Our Daily Bread" in *Becoming a Praying Congregation*, 84.)

Taking Time to Reflect

 Pause and recall what you have read and heard, as well as your own life experiences. Take note of anything that particularly catches your attention—perhaps a word, phrase, or image.

Making Our Requests Known

Focus your prayers more specifically on particular things, persons, or circumstances. The following petitions offer guidance:

Prayers for God's Creation and Our World
Prayers for All God's People
Prayers for the Church and All Who Seek God
Prayers for Our Neighbors
Prayers for Our Families and Friends
Prayers for Ourselves

Thanking God for Our Prayers and Life

The LORD is my shepherd.
    I lack nothing.
He lets me rest in grassy meadows;
        he leads me to restful waters;
            he keeps me alive.
He guides me in proper paths
        for the sake of his good name. (Psalm 23:1-3)

Prayer at the End of the Day

Inviting God's Activity

Tender Shepherd of my soul, make yourself and your way known to me in this evening time of prayer and reflection. By the power of your presence, bring me to the end of the day whole, complete, and at peace with you, my neighbor, and myself. Grant a night of peaceful rest and send me forth tomorrow as a witness to your love and grace.

A Continuing Request

Create a clean heart for me, God;
> put a new, faithful spirit deep inside me! (Psalm 51:10)

Gathering the Day

Remembering—Reflect on the day's experiences.

Confessing—Own up to your own weakness, failure, and sin.

Forgiving —Ask for and accept God's forgiveness, and forgive yourself and all who may have injured you or those you love.

Thanksgiving—Give thanks for the gifts that God has granted this day.

Offering

My whole being clings to you;
> your strong hand upholds me. (Psalm 63:8)

Blessing

I will lie down and fall asleep in peace
> because you alone, LORD, let me live in safety. (Psalm 4:8)

Week 11

The Way Disciples Live

Approaching God with Intention

Creator God
Whose name is love,
Who made all that is
And is creating still,

Speak to me now as I listen
   for your word of truth,
For I am yours and desire to
Live as your faithful child this day
   and always.

 Sit in silence and stillness for a few moments, lengthening the time each day as you are able.

Becoming Aware of God's Presence

> You are my secret hideout!
> > You protect me from trouble.
> > You surround me with songs of rescue! (Psalm 32:7)

Inviting God's Intervention

> Please protect my life! Deliver me!
> > Don't let me be put to shame
> > because I take refuge in you.
> Let integrity and virtue guard me
> > because I hope in you. (Psalm 25:20-21)

Listening for God's Voice

Open yourself to hear what God is saying to you through the Scriptures.

"You are the salt of the earth. But if salt loses its saltiness, how will it become salty again? It's good for nothing except to be thrown away and trampled under people's feet. You are the light of the world. A city on top of a hill can't be hidden. Neither do people light a lamp and put it under a basket. Instead, they put it on top of a lampstand, and it shines on all who are in the house. In the same way, let your light shine before people, so they can see the good things you do and praise your Father who is in heaven.

"Don't even begin to think that I have come to do away with the Law and the Prophets. I haven't come to do away with them but to fulfill them. I say to you very seriously that as long as heaven and earth exist, neither the smallest letter nor even the smallest stroke of a pen will be erased from the Law until everything there becomes a reality. Therefore, whoever ignores one of the least of these commands and teaches others to do the same will be called the lowest in the kingdom of heaven. But whoever keeps these commands and teaches people to keep them will be called great in the kingdom of heaven. I say to you that unless your righteousness is greater than the righteousness of the legal experts and the Pharisees, you will never enter the kingdom of heaven. (Matthew 5:13-20)

Alternative Readings

Luke 9:57-62

Isaiah 6:1-8

Matthew 18:1-5

1 Corinthians 2:1-12

Micah 6:6-8

Luke 12:22-34

Practicing Spiritual Reading

As you read the essay and one or more quotations each day, do so with an openness for further contemplation on the week's theme. Ask God, Is there a word or prayer for my life in these words?

Living with Jesus is not easy. It never was. Even a casual reading of the Gospels shakes us up because they make it clear that living as a disciple brings earthshaking challenges. Jesus was physically with the first disciples to coach, teach, mentor, encourage, guide, protect, and provide. Still these early disciples were often perplexed, uncertain, and fearful. There were times when they just didn't get it.

The way Jesus plunged across boundaries and accepted everyone where they were was enough to keep them off balance as they tried to understand and keep up with their leader. Of course there were other times when they were filled with exuberance, confidence, courage, integrity, understanding, and strength. Those times when they rose to the challenge of living as a faithful disciple of Jesus.

In our deepest and best moments, that is the way we would like to live all the time. But when those complacency-shattering requests come, the ones that shatter our comfortable boundaries, we, too, get nervous, unsettled, and sometimes very much afraid. The good news is that Jesus still comes to us in the power and presence of the Holy Spirit to help us understand and to give us all the strength we need to prevail as faithful disciples. All we need to do is ask.

Today, when those complacency-shattering requests come that seem impossible to fulfill, Jesus is still with us through the power and presence of the Holy Spirit to offer to us the help we need to live faithfully as a follower of Jesus.

 Overwork is the biggest obstacle to seekers moving toward the kind of prayer that is absorption into God beyond images. We need an environment that will image back to us all that is or is not of God. This is why a cell is a sacred place that is kept deliberately simple. . . . The cell is really the secret closet that Matthew talks about where we talk to our

Father in secret (Matt. 6:6). It's not really a place or a time after awhile, but an act of descending the mind into the heart and dwelling there. All of us need an external mechanism to protect our internal world. (Funk, *Tools Matter for Practicing the Spiritual Life*, 70–71.)

It is impossible to live in close communion with any person and not take on some of the qualities of that person. So it is with Jesus Christ. To live with Jesus is to begin to take on the qualities that marked his life. Unqualified love for and obedience to God, unconditional love of neighbor, and a radical selflessness were an integral part of the life and ministry of Jesus. To follow Jesus is to incorporate these qualities into our lives as well. (Job, *A Wesleyan Spiritual Reader*, 76.)

When we pray for others, we not only seek something for them but we also acknowledge our dependency on them. We only achieve being through relationships with others, with other real persons. A glimpse of this mystery and its fundamental reality appears in the image of the Trinity. The internal being of God exists as relationship, a love so vital and vividly expressed that only the image of persons in unceasing connection to each other can capture it. (Ulanov, *Primary Speech*, 85–86.)

Taking Time to Reflect

Pause and recall what you have read and heard, as well as your own life experiences. Take note of anything that particularly catches your attention—perhaps a word, phrase, or image.

Making Our Requests Known

Focus your prayers more specifically on particular things, persons, or circumstances. The following petitions offer guidance:

Prayers for God's Creation and Our World
Prayers for All God's People
Prayers for the Church and All Who Seek God
Prayers for Our Neighbors
Prayers for Our Families and Friends
Prayers for Ourselves

Thanking God for Our Prayers and Life

Faithful Guide and Companion,
continue to speak to me the words of guidance,
correction, encouragement, and love that I need.
And send me to meet this day
with your power and presence
to go where Jesus Christ leads me
and live as your faithful disciple all day long.

Prayer at the End of the Day

Inviting God's Activity

Tender Shepherd of my soul, make yourself and your way known to me in this evening time of prayer and reflection. By the power of your presence, bring me to the end of the day whole, complete, and at peace with you, my neighbor, and myself. Grant a night of peaceful rest and send me forth tomorrow as a witness to your love and grace.

A Continuing Request

Create a clean heart for me, God;
   put a new, faithful spirit deep inside me! (Psalm 51:10)

Gathering the Day

Remembering—Reflect on the day's experiences.

Confessing—Own up to your own weakness, failure, and sin.

Forgiving—Ask for and accept God's forgiveness, and forgive yourself and all who may have injured you or those you love.

Thanksgiving—Give thanks for the gifts that God has granted this day.

Offering

My whole being clings to you;
   your strong hand upholds me. (Psalm 63:8)

Blessing

I will lie down and fall asleep in peace
   because you alone, LORD, let me live in safety. (Psalm 4:8)

Week 12

In Need of Healing

Approaching God with Intention

God, you have ordered that your decrees
   should be kept most carefully.
How I wish my ways were strong
   when it comes to keeping your statutes!
Then I wouldn't be ashamed
   when I examine all your commandments.
I will give thanks to you with a heart that does right
   as I learn your righteous rules.
I will keep your statutes.
      Please don't leave me all alone! (Psalm 119:4-8)

 Sit in silence and stillness for a few moments, lengthening the time each day as you are able.

Becoming Aware of God's Presence

Heaven is declaring God's glory;
   the sky is proclaiming his handiwork.
One day gushes the news to the next,
   and one night informs another what needs to be known.
                                    (Psalm 19:1-2)

Inviting God's Intervention

So now you, LORD—
>don't hold back any of your compassion from me.
Let your loyal love and faithfulness always protect me.
>>>(Psalm 40:11)

Listening for God's Voice

Open yourself to hear what God is saying to you through the Scriptures.

Therefore, after you have gotten rid of lying, *Each of you must tell the truth to your neighbor* because we are parts of each other in the same body. *Be angry without sinning.* Don't let the sun set on your anger. Don't provide an opportunity for the devil. Thieves should no longer steal. Instead, they should go to work, using their hands to do good so that they will have something to share with whoever is in need.

Don't let any foul words come out of your mouth. Only say what is helpful when it is needed for building up the community so that it benefits those who hear what you say. Don't make the Holy Spirit of God unhappy—you were sealed by him for the day of redemption. Put aside all bitterness, losing your temper, anger, shouting, and slander, along with every other evil. Be kind, compassionate, and forgiving to each other, in the same way God forgave you in Christ. (Ephesians 4:25-32)

Alternative Readings

Job 29:1-20

Matthew 4:23-25

Acts 3:1-10

1 Corinthians 3:1-9

Matthew 8:1-4

Psalm 1

Practicing Spiritual Reading

As you read the essay and one or more quotations each day, do so with an openness for further contemplation on the week's theme. Ask God, Is there a word or prayer for my life in these words?

Sitting in a crowded waiting room of a large university medical center, I was struck by the great variety of persons in the room. Some very old who needed assistance to walk and some very young who were being carried and with nearly every color of skin represented. I assumed the one thing they had in common was that they wanted to be healed of whatever ailment brought them there. Waiting for my name to be called, I thought of the experience of Jesus at the pool in Jerusalem as it is told in John 5:2-9. The "clinic at the pool" was also crowded when Jesus approached and spoke to a man who had been ill for thirty-eight years. It is not surprising that Jesus, who seemed to show compassion to everyone he met, spoke to the person who had been there so long seeking a cure.

The surprising thing is that Jesus asked him if he wanted to be made well. What a silly question. Everyone wants to be made well. This man had been there seeking healing for what must have seemed like a lifetime and in response to the question, "Do you want to be healed?" he replies that he has no one to help him get into the healing water at the right time. Jesus then tells him to "Stand up, take your mat and walk." I wondered what the doctor would tell each of the persons in the waiting room and what she would tell me. How much of my well-being is up to me? What must I do to appropriate God's life-giving power in my life?

 If you are feeling a loss of the awareness of God's presence, one of the most helpful things to do is to learn about the lives of some of the great lovers of God through history. Or learn about someone who has been transformed by God in this present time. The person need not be a great saint or mystic. He or she could be some ordinary person (are there any ordinary persons?) whom you know, one who has experienced God and whose life has been changed through that encounter. (Flora Slosson Wuellner, *Heart of Healing, Heart of Light: Encountering God, Who Shares and Heals Our Pain*, na.)

Not only is it impossible to step outside God's gracious reach, but God is always actively engaged on our behalf. God's right hand does hold us fast, no matter how far we stray from God's grand design for us, a design that was in place even before the foundation of the world (Job, *A Wesleyan Spiritual Reader*, 108.)

One of the basic consequences of living as a Christian is coming to know ourselves. That entails both struggle and joy. It is a lifetime task that leads to wholeness not only within ourselves but in our perception of all of the reality that surrounds us. It is this integration that makes it possible for us not only to call Jesus' name, but to accept the consequences. We will be called to submit to the fire and be transformed, to climb mountains and to relax in the cool valley by a refreshing stream. The slopes and the upgrades of our lives will alternate, but we will have the constant reassurance of following one who loves us and knows how to set the pace. (Carole Marie Kelly, *Symbols of Inner Truth: Uncovering the Spiritual Meaning of Experience*, 48.)

We should not be surprised or scandalized by the sinful and the tragic. Do what you can to *be* peace and to *do* justice, but never expect or demand perfection on this earth. It usually leads to a false moral outrage, a negative identity, intolerance, paranoia, and self-serving crusades against "the contaminating element," instead of "becoming a new creation" ourselves (Gal. 6:15). (Rohr, *Everything Belongs*, 179.)

Taking Time to Reflect

 Pause and recall what you have read and heard, as well as your own life experiences. Take note of anything that particularly catches your attention—perhaps a word, phrase, or image.

Making Our Requests Known

Focus your prayers more specifically on particular things, persons, or circumstances. The following petitions offer guidance:

Prayers for God's Creation and Our World
Prayers for All God's People
Prayers for the Church and All Who Seek God
Prayers for Our Neighbors
Prayers for Our Families and Friends
Prayers for Ourselves

Thanking God for Our Prayers and Life

> Let my whole being bless the LORD!
> > Let everything inside me bless his holy name!
> Let my whole being bless the LORD
> > and never forget all his good deeds:
> > how God forgives all your sins,
> > heals all your sickness,
> > saves your life from the pit,
> > crowns you with faithful love and compassion,
> > and satisfies you with plenty of good things
> > > so that your youth is made fresh like an eagle's.
> > > > (Psalm 103:1-5)

Prayer at the End of the Day

Inviting God's Activity

Tender Shepherd of my soul, make yourself and your way known to me in this evening time of prayer and reflection. By the power of your presence, bring me to the end of the day whole, complete, and at peace with you, my neighbor, and myself. Grant a night of peaceful rest and send me forth tomorrow as a witness to your love and grace.

A Continuing Request

Create a clean heart for me, God;
> put a new, faithful spirit deep inside me! (Psalm 51:10)

Gathering the Day

Remembering—Reflect on the day's experiences.

Confessing—Own up to your own weakness, failure, and sin.

Forgiving—Ask for and accept God's forgiveness, and forgive yourself and all who may have injured you or those you love.

Thanksgiving—Give thanks for the gifts that God has granted this day.

Offering

My whole being clings to you;
> your strong hand upholds me. (Psalm 63:8)

Blessing

I will lie down and fall asleep in peace
> because you alone, LORD, let me live in safety. (Psalm 4:8)

Week 13

Looking for the Right Way

Approaching God with Intention

God of promise,
power,
and presence,
be my ever-present Companion
and Guide
so that this day and always
I may be your faithful servant child.

 Sit in silence and stillness for a few moments, lengthening the time each day as you are able.

Becoming Aware of God's Presence

Living in the Most High's shelter,
    camping in the Almighty's shade,
I say to the LORD, "You are my refuge, my stronghold!
    You are my God—the one I trust!" (Psalm 91:1-2)

Inviting God's Intervention

I've taken refuge in you, LORD.
    Don't let me ever be put to shame!
Deliver me and rescue me by your righteousness!

Bend your ear toward me and save me!
Be my rock of refuge
    where I can always escape.
You commanded that my life be saved
    because you are my rock and my fortress. (Psalm 71:1-3)

Listening for God's Voice

Open yourself to hear what God is saying to you through the Scriptures.

"But I say to you who are willing to hear: Love your enemies. Do good to those who hate you. Bless those who curse you. Pray for those who mistreat you. If someone slaps you on the cheek, offer the other one as well. If someone takes your coat, don't withhold your shirt either. Give to everyone who asks and don't demand your things back from those who take them. Treat people in the same way that you want them to treat you.

"If you love those who love you, why should you be commended? Even sinners love those who love them. If you do good to those who do good to you, why should you be commended? Even sinners do that. If you lend to those from whom you expect repayment, why should you be commended? Even sinners lend to sinners expecting to be paid back in full. Instead, love your enemies, do good, and lend expecting nothing in return. If you do, you will have a great reward. You will be acting the way children of the Most High act, for he is kind to ungrateful and wicked people. Be compassionate just as your Father is compassionate.

"Don't judge, and you won't be judged. Don't condemn, and you won't be condemned. Forgive, and you will be forgiven. Give, and it will be given to you. A good portion—packed down, firmly shaken, and overflowing—will fall into your lap. The portion you give will determine the portion you receive in return." (Luke 6:27-38)

Alternative Readings

Genesis 45:3-11
Romans 8:18-27
Matthew 7:15-20
Leviticus 19:1-2, 9-18
Galatians 5:13-15
Galatians 5:16-26

Practicing Spiritual Reading

As you read the essay and one or more quotations each day, do so with an openness for further contemplation on the week's theme. Ask God, Is there a word or prayer for my life in these words?

We have seen too much hate and too much violence in word and action. Deep in our hearts we know there is a better way, and deep in our hearts we want to follow that way always. We begin that way by remembering who God is and who we are as God's children. With these truths deeply imbedded in our lives, we, too, can decide to walk the way of love, justice, reconciliation, and peace because we want to walk in companionship with the One who is love and who calls us to love God and neighbor.

There is wisdom in the ancient story of a wise mentor who asked his students if they could tell when darkness was leaving and the light was coming. They gave many answers and finally gave up seeking the answer their mentor was helping them discover. The wise mentor then responded, "We know the darkness is leaving and the dawn is coming when we can see another person and know that this is our brother or our sister; otherwise, no matter what time it is, it is still dark" (Foster, *Prayer*, 249).

We are children of the light, children of God; and when we claim our full inheritance as children of God, we are able to see clearly and to know in the depth of our being that when we look at another human being, we are looking at a sister or brother who is God's beloved child, just as we are. When this happens, we see ourselves as we are and then are able to see others as they are. (Job, *Three Simple Questions*, 43–44.)

 God is present, hoping, and urging, in the midst of all the situations of life. As Christians, we believe that God is passionately involved in human affairs and intimately invested in all our questioning. Moreover, we believe that God's involvement in our lives has purpose and direction. God is seeking to bring healing and wholeness and reconciliation, transforming this broken world into that New Creation where there will be no more sadness or injustice or pain. Our decisions and our search for guidance take place in the active presence of a God who intimately cares about our life situations and who invites us to participate in the divine activities of healing and transformation. (Frank Rogers Jr., "Discernment" in *Practicing Our Faith: A Way of Life for a Searching People,* 106.)

In modern life we have become so busy with our daily affairs and thoughts that we have forgotten this essential art of taking time to converse with our heart. When we ask it about our current path, we must look at the values we have chosen to live by. Where do we put our time, our strength, our creativity, our love? We must look at our life without sentimentality, exaggeration, or idealism. Does what we are choosing reflect what we most deeply value? (Jack Kornfield, *A Path with Heart: A Guide Through the Perils and Promises of Spiritual Life*, 12.)

The power by which God transforms humans is the Holy Spirit. Christian spirituality is therefore not a matter of cultivating some dimension of the human spirit, but a matter of obedient response to the Spirit of God. (Luke Timothy Johnson, *The Creed: What Christians Believe and Why It Matters*, 245.)

I have often found myself clinging to the words and the message of passages such as Hebrews 13:5-6, *"I will never leave you or forsake you."* So we can say with confidence, *"The Lord is my helper; I will not be afraid. What can anyone do to me?"* [NRSV] Yes, I have reached out again and again, needing and always finding the strong arm and guiding hand of God available for one who seeks. (Job, *Life Stories*, 76.)

Taking Time to Reflect

 Pause and recall what you have read and heard, as well as your own life experiences. Take note of anything that particularly catches your attention—perhaps a word, phrase, or image.

Making Our Requests Known

Focus your prayers more specifically on particular things, persons, or circumstances. The following petitions offer guidance:

Prayers for God's Creation and Our World
Prayers for All God's People
Prayers for the Church and All Who Seek God
Prayers for Our Neighbors
Prayers for Our Families and Friends
Prayers for Ourselves

Thanking God for Our Prayers and Life

God of love, holiness, and strength,
we thank you for the gift of your presence
through the morning hours.
Continue to make yourself
and your way
known to us throughout the remaining hours
of the day.
Grant us grace to follow you
in faithfulness, joy, and peace.
We are yours.

Prayer at the End of the Day

Inviting God's Activity

Tender Shepherd of my soul, make yourself and your way known to me in this evening time of prayer and reflection. By the power of your presence, bring me to the end of the day whole, complete, and at peace with you, my neighbor, and myself. Grant a night of peaceful rest and send me forth tomorrow as a witness to your love and grace.

A Continuing Request

Create a clean heart for me, God;
    put a new, faithful spirit deep inside me! (Psalm 51:10)

Gathering the Day

Remembering—Reflect on the day's experiences.

Confessing—Own up to your own weakness, failure, and sin.

Forgiving—Ask for and accept God's forgiveness, and forgive yourself and all who may have injured you or those you love.

Thanksgiving—Give thanks for the gifts that God has granted this day.

Offering

My whole being clings to you;
    your strong hand upholds me. (Psalm 63:8)

Blessing

I will lie down and fall asleep in peace
    because you alone, LORD, let me live in safety. (Psalm 4:8)

Week 14

Jesus as Our Teacher

Approaching God with Intention

O Divine Love,
who calls and sends all who follow you,
help me in this time apart
to once more hear your voice.
Grant grace to hear your voice
calling and sending me,
and grant faith enough
to respond in obedience.
Amen.

 Sit in silence and stillness for a few moments, lengthening the time each day as you are able.

Becoming Aware of God's Presence

> LORD, you have been our help,
>   generation after generation.
> Before the mountains were born,
>   before you birthed the earth and the inhabited world—
>   from forever in the past
>   to forever in the future, you are God. (Psalm 90:1-2)

Inviting God's Intervention

> Teach me to do what pleases you,
>   because you are my God.
> Guide me by your good spirit
>   into good land. (Psalm 143:10)

Listening for God's Voice

Open yourself to hear what God is saying to you through the Scriptures.

> Jesus and his followers went into Capernaum. Immediately on the Sabbath Jesus entered the synagogue and started teaching. The people were amazed by his teaching, for he was teaching them with authority, not like the legal experts. Suddenly, there in the synagogue, a person with an evil spirit screamed, "What have you to do with us, Jesus of Nazareth? Have you come to destroy us? I know who you are. You are the holy one from God."
>
> "Silence!" Jesus said, speaking harshly to the demon. "Come out of him!" The unclean spirit shook him and screamed, then it came out.
>
> Everyone was shaken and questioned among themselves, "What's this? A new teaching with authority! He even commands unclean spirits and they obey him!" Right away the news about him spread throughout the entire region of Galilee. (Mark 1:21-28)

Alternative Readings

Micah 4:1-5
2 Corinthians 3:1-6
John 7:10-24
Matthew 6:24-34
Matthew 23:1-12
Luke 6:39-49

Practicing Spiritual Reading

As you read the essay and one or more quotations each day, do so with an openness for further contemplation on the week's theme. Ask God, Is there a word or prayer for my life in these words?

Jesus the master teacher surprises us with the easy way he offers earthshaking principles and a revolutionary way of life. For the most part we have tamed those teachings to something we can tolerate without too much embarrassment at our failure to actually practice what Jesus lived and taught. But in our better moments we do want to be like Jesus, live like Jesus, and die like Jesus. Well, maybe we do sometimes, but we like to choose the times and the places.

But upon closer examination, we realize that even though Jesus lived a pretty risky life, challenging the religious authority as well as the cultural wisdom of his day, we do want to live like him and be like him. When we sit with and walk with this master teacher, we will be taught new ways of living and of being. And if we have the courage to continue in the presence of this master teacher, we may find our lives transformed more and more into that divine image that we all carry deep within, although sometimes hidden behind our fears. May we spend this day in the classroom with Jesus.

 Now disciples of Jesus are people who want to take into their being the order of The Kingdom Among Us. They wish to live their life in it as Jesus himself would, and that requires internalization of that order. Study is the chief way in which they do it. They devote their attention, their thoughtful inquiry, and their practical experimentation to the order of the kingdom as seen in Jesus, in the written word of Scripture, in others who walk in the way, and, indeed, in every good thing in nature, history, and culture. (Dallas Willard, *The Divine Conspiracy: Rediscovering Our Hidden Life in God*, 361.)

They asked Jesus, "Show us the Father." And in response, he portrayed a messy, divine recklessness at the very heart of reality:

A farmer went out to sow and he . . . carefully prepared the soil, removing all rocks and weeds, marking off neat rows, placing each seed exactly six inches from the other, covering each with three-quarters of soil?

No. This sower just began slinging seed. Seed everywhere. Some fell on the path, some on the rocks, some in weeds, and some, miraculously, fell on good soil, took root, and rendered harvest. That's what the Word of God is like, said Jesus. (William H. Willimon, "The Messiness of Ministry," *Princeton Seminary Bulletin* 14, 231.)

A further consequence of life in Christ is the pursuit of the way of Christ. We seek to be faithful and obedient as Jesus Christ was obedient. We observe more closely the life of Jesus and try to incorporate his ways into our own. As we do this, we learn to love God and realize that we cannot truly love God without loving our neighbor. (Job, *A Wesleyan Spiritual Reader*, 37.)

Taking Time to Reflect

 Pause and recall what you have read and heard, as well as your own life experiences. Take note of anything that particularly catches your attention—perhaps a word, phrase, or image.

Making Our Requests Known

Focus your prayers more specifically on particular things, persons, or circumstances. The following petitions offer guidance:

Prayers for God's Creation and Our World
Prayers for All God's People
Prayers for the Church and All Who Seek God
Prayers for Our Neighbors
Prayers for Our Families and Friends
Prayers for Ourselves

Thanking God for Our Prayers and Life

Make your ways known to me, LORD;
　　teach me your paths.
Lead me in your truth—teach it to me—
　　because you are the God who saves me.
　　　　I put my hope in you all day long.
LORD, remember your compassion and faithful love—
　　they are forever!
But don't remember the sins of my youth or my wrongdoing.
　　Remember me only according to your faithful love
　　　　for the sake of your goodness, LORD. (Psalm 25:4-7)

Prayer at the End of the Day

Inviting God's Activity

Tender Shepherd of my soul, make yourself and your way known to me in this evening time of prayer and reflection. By the power of your presence, bring me to the end of the day whole, complete, and at peace with you, my neighbor, and myself. Grant a night of peaceful rest and send me forth tomorrow as a witness to your love and grace.

A Continuing Request

Create a clean heart for me, God;
    put a new, faithful spirit deep inside me! (Psalm 51:10)

Gathering the Day

Remembering—Reflect on the day's experiences.

Confessing—Own up to your own weakness, failure, and sin.

Forgiving—Ask for and accept God's forgiveness, and forgive yourself and all who may have injured you or those you love.

Thanksgiving—Give thanks for the gifts that God has granted this day.

Offering

My whole being clings to you;
    your strong hand upholds me. (Psalm 63:8)

Blessing

I will lie down and fall asleep in peace
    because you alone, LORD, let me live in safety. (Psalm 4:8)

Prayer Practice

Silence and Stillness

As we seek to listen and pray in a noisy world, it is appropriate and necessary to learn to sit in silence and stillness. Sitting in silence helps to prepare our hearts and minds for communion with God, allowing us to become more aware of God's presence with us. You are encouraged to make the practice of sitting in silence and stillness a focal part of your prayer time.

Begin by sitting quietly and comfortably. Allow the exterior voices to be silenced as you focus on the interior voice of God, who is seeking your attention. Some use a physical item such as a cross or icon to assist them in reaching this place of silence where the gentle voice of God's spirit may be heard, understood, and obeyed. If your mind wanders or you are distracted, gently return your focus to God's interior voice.

With persistence and practice, sitting in silence and stillness will become more and more comfortable and natural, and you will look forward to this time of quieting your soul before God. (Job, *Listen*, 22.)

Week 15

Listening to Jesus

Approaching God with Intention

Holy God,
Speak to me gently and clearly,
    for I am yours
    and desire to hear, understand,
    and be obedient
    to your slightest whisper.
Speak, for I am listening.

 Sit in silence and stillness for a few moments, lengthening the time each day as you are able.

Becoming Aware of God's Presence

Then a voice from the cloud said, "This is my Son, my chosen one. Listen to him!" (Luke 9:35)

Inviting God's Intervention

I will never forget your precepts
    because through them you gave me life again.
I'm yours—save me
    because I've pursued your precepts! (Psalm 119:93-94)

Listening for God's Voice

Open yourself to hear what God is saying to you through the Scriptures.

> Six days later Jesus took Peter, James, and John his brother, and brought them to the top of a very high mountain. He was transformed in front of them. His face shone like the sun, and his clothes became as white as light.
>
> Moses and Elijah appeared to them, talking with Jesus. Peter reacted to all of this by saying to Jesus, "Lord, it's good that we're here. If you want, I'll make three shrines: one for you, one for Moses, and one for Elijah."
>
> While he was still speaking, look, a bright cloud overshadowed them. A voice from the cloud said, "This is my Son whom I dearly love. I am very pleased with him. Listen to him!" Hearing this, the disciples fell on their faces, filled with awe.
>
> But Jesus came and touched them. "Get up," he said. "Don't be afraid." When they looked up, they saw no one except Jesus.
>
> As they were coming down the mountain, Jesus commanded them, "Don't tell anybody about the vision until the Human One is raised from the dead." (Matthew 17:1-9)

Alternative Readings

Luke 11:27-28
Isaiah 42:1-9
Hebrews 3:7-15
John 10:1-6
Acts 13:44-52
Acts 28:23-31

Practicing Spiritual Reading

As you read the essay and one or more quotations each day, do so with an openness for further contemplation on the week's theme. Ask God, Is there a word or prayer for my life in these words?

It is difficult to follow Jesus if we do not know where he is going and where he wants to lead us. The voice from the cloud told those first disciples to listen to Jesus. I imagine the advice is true for us as well. It is so important for us to find ways of listening to what Jesus has to say to us today.

Of course this is true so that we may know what it means to follow Jesus, and it is also true so that we may find grace and strength to do so. We may not be able to open our lives to the amazing grace that is available to guide us, sustain us, comfort us, and keep us unless we listen to hear where Jesus is leading us. So we learn to listen so that we will not miss the most important voice of all time with the most important message we will ever hear.

Jesus often sought silence and solitude to pray and seek his beloved Abba's direction. No matter where we are in our busy and noisy world, we can do the same, but it will take practice, patience, and perseverance. . . .

Our greatest challenge will be to learn to listen to the many ways in which God is speaking to us all the time—through Scripture, creation, history, current events, the stories of others and of our own lives, and the moments of our daily existence—and then to trust that the Holy Spirit desires to guide us as we learn how to pray and discern God's purpose and will for us in every situation. (Job, *Listen*, 11-13.)

Prayer . . . is for the reception of identity one more time so that we do not forget who we are and who we are called to be. It is for sons and daughters returning one more time to the parent to receive our birthright. And in prayer, we have to do with this parent who says, "you are my daughter," "you are my son." And then we are empowered to decide what that identity and relationship mean and how we shall live out our lives. . . . Such practice of prayer leaves us authored, because we have to do with the One who is our author. (Walter Brueggemann, "Covenantal Spirituality," in *New Conversations*, 8, quoted in Job, *Three Simple Questions*, 45–46.)

Standing in the silence we do not need to be convinced of its reality. But we do need to be reminded of another reality. . . . We are given signs and songs even in the darkest night, signs and songs that assure us of the presence of the only One who can shatter our silence. . . . Even the darkness and the silence lose their fearful quality and the questions that haunt us are seen as insignificant in the light of God's mighty deeds in Jesus Christ. We begin to learn, even in the silence, that God continues to love us, guide us, and care for us. (Job, *A Guide to Retreat*, 21.)

Taking Time to Reflect

 Pause and recall what you have read and heard, as well as your own life experiences. Take note of anything that particularly catches your attention—perhaps a word, phrase, or image.

Making Our Requests Known

Focus your prayers more specifically on particular things, persons, or circumstances. The following petitions offer guidance:

Prayers for God's Creation and Our World
Prayers for All God's People
Prayers for the Church and All Who Seek God
Prayers for Our Neighbors
Prayers for Our Families and Friends
Prayers for Ourselves

Thanking God for Our Prayers and Life

Loving God,
I offer to you all that I am
All that I hope to become
And invite your transforming presence
To shape me more and more into your
Beloved and faithful child
For I am yours and I belong to you
My faithful Savior and Guide.

Prayer at the End of the Day

Inviting God's Activity

Tender Shepherd of my soul, make yourself and your way known to me in this evening time of prayer and reflection. By the power of your presence, bring me to the end of the day whole, complete, and at peace with you, my neighbor, and myself. Grant a night of peaceful rest and send me forth tomorrow as a witness to your love and grace.

A Continuing Request

Create a clean heart for me, God;
     put a new, faithful spirit deep inside me! (Psalm 51:10)

Gathering the Day

Remembering – Reflect on the day's experiences.

Confessing – Own up to your own weakness, failure, and sin.

Forgiving – Ask for and accept God's forgiveness, and forgive yourself and all who may have injured you or those you love.

Thanksgiving – Give thanks for the gifts that God has granted this day.

Offering

My whole being clings to you;
     your strong hand upholds me. (Psalm 63:8)

Blessing

I will lie down and fall asleep in peace
     because you alone, LORD, let me live in safety. (Psalm 4:8)

Week 16

Learning Who We Are

Approaching God with Intention

LORD, you have examined me.
    You know me.
You know when I sit down and when I stand up.
    Even from far away, you comprehend my plans.
You study my traveling and resting.
    You are thoroughly familiar with all my ways.
There isn't a word on my tongue, LORD,
    that you don't already know completely.
You surround me—front and back.
    You put your hand on me. . . .

Examine me, God! Look at my heart!
    Put me to the test! Know my anxious thoughts!
Look to see if there is any idolatrous way in me,
    then lead me on the eternal path! (Psalm 139:1-5, 23-24)

   *Sit in silence and stillness for a few moments, lengthening the time
    each day as you are able.*

Becoming Aware of God's Presence

So what are we going to say about these things? If God is for us,
who is against us? He didn't spare his own Son but gave him up

for us all. Won't he also freely give us all things with him?

(Romans 8:31-32)

Inviting God's Intervention

LORD, show us favor;
>   we hope in you.
Be our strength every morning,
>   our salvation in times of distress. (Isaiah 33:2)

Listening for God's Voice

Open yourself to hear what God is saying to you through the Scriptures.

Dear friends, don't be surprised about the fiery trials that have come among you to test you. These are not strange happenings. Instead, rejoice as you share Christ's suffering. You share his suffering now so that you may also have overwhelming joy when his glory is revealed. If you are mocked because of Christ's name, you are blessed, for the Spirit of glory—indeed, the Spirit of God—rests on you.

Now none of you should suffer as a murderer or thief or evildoer or rebel. But don't be ashamed if you suffer as one who belongs to Christ. Rather, honor God as you bear Christ's name. Give honor to God, because it's time for judgment to begin with God's own household. But if judgment starts with us, what will happen to those who refuse to believe God's good news? If the righteous are barely rescued, what will happen to the godless and sinful? So then, those who suffer because they follow God's will should commit their lives to a trustworthy creator by doing what is right. (1 Peter 4:12-19)

Alternative Readings

2 Samuel 23:1-4

2 Corinthians 4:1-15

Luke 22:39-46

James 1:12-18

Genesis 9:8-17

Psalm 139:13-18

Practicing Spiritual Reading

As you read the essay and one or more quotations each day, do so with an openness for further contemplation on the week's theme. Ask God, Is there a word or prayer for my life in these words?

Far too often we witness national and global tragedies that result in death and wounding of many. We also have seen political leaders divide communities, states, and nations by their rhetoric and actions. It is not a time to offer excuses or to place blame. But it is time for all Christians to remember who we are and to chart and follow a new path—a path that always moves away from violence and toward peace, a path that leads us away from the implied and symbolic threat of much of our national discourse, a path that affirms finding a way forward that benefits all and not just a few, a path that is in harmony with the One we claim as Lord and Savior, Jesus Christ, a path that I believe we all want to follow.

In this world darkened by confusion, deception, and dysfunction, it is easy to forget who we are. Even in our affluent nation, the tension, hurry, competitiveness, and false idols that surround us bring enormous stress to our identity as individuals. We struggle to remember who we are, and in our age of instant and constant communication, it becomes easy to attach labels to each other—and so difficult to put them away. It is often hard for us to see beyond a label and discover the beloved child of God who has been hidden by another's unfortunate choice of words or actions. (Job, *Three Simple Questions*, 40–41).

In Jesus we have the best picture of who God is, how God acts in the world, and how God relates to us. In Jesus we discover the truth that you and I are God's beloved children, just like every other person on this good earth. We not only are "authored" by God; we are sustained by God every moment of our existence. Our destiny is to live in confidence and trust in loving relationship with this mighty God and with our neighbors—with all God's children—who are just like you and me. When we begin to live this way, we begin to love as God loves;

we begin to love our neighbors as we love ourselves. (Job, *Three Simple Questions*, 55.)

Jesus teaches others to call God *Abba*, encouraging them to trust God the way little children trust a good parent to take care of them, be compassionate over their weakness, and stand guard against those who would harm them. Jesus' *Abba* experience is the heart of the matter, the dynamism behind his preaching the reign of God and of his typical way of acting. God *Abba* was the passion of his life. (Elizabeth A. Johnson, *Consider Jesus: Waves of Renewal in Christology*, 57.)

Integrity involves wholeness and authenticity. It is living a life consistent with who I am within. It is living a life that requires my thoughts, my feelings and my actions to be congruent, to be the union of who I am within—what I believe, who I understand myself to be and how I live my life. (Ronald J. Greer, *If You Know Who You Are, You Will Know What to Do: Living with Integrity*, 17.)

In the first three centuries, the training of Christian leaders occurred on the job.... [The disciples] learned the significance of prayer or other acts of symbolic devotion, therefore, from seeing them in the life of Jesus, an observant Jew with a strong divine consciousness. If we may trust the impression left by the Synoptic Gospels, Jesus implanted in their minds the necessity of a profound God-awareness in all of life that was to be sharpened by prayer and other acts of worship. (E. Glenn Hinson, *Spiritual Preparation for Christian Leadership*, 15–16.)

Taking Time to Reflect

Pause and recall what you have read and heard, as well as your own life experiences. Take note of anything that particularly catches your attention—perhaps a word, phrase, or image.

Making Our Requests Known

Focus your prayers more specifically on particular things, persons, or circumstances. The following petitions offer guidance:

Prayers for God's Creation and Our World
Prayers for All God's People

Prayers for the Church and All Who Seek God
Prayers for Our Neighbors
Prayers for Our Families and Friends
Prayers for Ourselves

Thanking God for Our Prayers and Life

Here am I, your loving creature,
offering all that I am
and hope to become to you,
my loving Creator.

Accept the gift I bring
and make it fruitful
as you keep me faithful,
for I am yours.

Prayer at the End of the Day

Inviting God's Activity

Tender Shepherd of my soul, make yourself and your way known to me in this evening time of prayer and reflection. By the power of your presence, bring me to the end of the day whole, complete, and at peace with you, my neighbor, and myself. Grant a night of peaceful rest and send me forth tomorrow as a witness to your love and grace.

A Continuing Request

Create a clean heart for me, God;
    put a new, faithful spirit deep inside me! (Psalm 51:10)

Gathering the Day

Remembering—Reflect on the day's experiences.

Confessing—Own up to your own weakness, failure, and sin.

Forgiving—Ask for and accept God's forgiveness, and forgive yourself and all who may have injured you or those you love.

Thanksgiving—Give thanks for the gifts that God has granted this day.

Offering

My whole being clings to you;
    your strong hand upholds me. (Psalm 63:8)

Blessing

I will lie down and fall asleep in peace
    because you alone, Lord, let me live in safety. (Psalm 4:8)

Week 17

Discipleship Is Not Too Costly

Approaching God with Intention

O God of Mercy,
make yourself known to me in this hour.
Illumine and remove from my life
those sins and distractions that prevent me
from being attentive and faithful.
Grant to me in this time apart
faith, wisdom, and courage
to see and rejoice
in your promises for my future. Amen.

 Sit in silence and stillness for a few moments, lengthening the time each day as you are able.

Becoming Aware of God's Presence

Pursue the Lord and his strength;
    seek his face always!
Remember the wondrous works he has done,
    all his marvelous works,
        and the justice he declared (Psalm 105:4-5)

Inviting God's Intervention

I have sought you with all my heart.
> Don't let me stray from any of your commandments!
I keep your word close, in my heart,
> so that I won't sin against you.
You, Lord, are to be blessed!
> Teach me your statutes. (Psalm 119:10-12)

Listening for God's Voice

Open yourself to hear what God is saying to you through the Scriptures

Then Jesus began to teach his disciples: "The Human One must suffer many things and be rejected by the elders, chief priests, and the legal experts, and be killed, and then, after three days, rise from the dead." He said this plainly. But Peter took hold of Jesus and, scolding him, began to correct him. Jesus turned and looked at his disciples, then sternly corrected Peter: "Get behind me, Satan. You are not thinking God's thoughts but human thoughts."

After calling the crowd together with his disciples, Jesus said to them, "All who want to come after me must say no to themselves, take up their cross, and follow me. All who want to save their lives will lose them. But all who lose their lives because of me and because of the good news will save them. Why would people gain the whole world but lose their lives? What will people give in exchange for their lives? Whoever is ashamed of me and my words in this unfaithful and sinful generation, the Human One will be ashamed of that person when he comes in the Father's glory with the holy angels." (Mark 8:31-38)

Alternative Readings

Luke 14:25-33
Philippians 3:17–4:1
Acts 14:19-23
Mark 10:28-31
John 8:31-38
Matthew 16:24-28

Practicing Spiritual Reading

As you read the essay and one or more quotations each day, do so with an openness for further contemplation on the week's theme. Ask God, Is there a word or prayer for my life in these words?

Following Jesus in a world like ours is not all that easy. There are costs involved. And why would we think otherwise? Living as a radical child of God was not that easy for Jesus, either. And the twelve found the earth moved beneath their feet, too, as they tried to follow not only the teachings of Jesus, but Jesus himself. But they also noticed that those who did not follow Jesus not only felt the earth move beneath their feet, they saw their world come apart. The twelve discovered that the cost of being a disciple was so minimal compared to the benefit of being a disciple that, upon close examination, it was a no-brainer to choose to follow the One who alone could give the gift of constant companionship with the living God in this world and the next. In a world like ours, only a life fully given to God can find fulfillment, security, a deep and abiding peace, and the intimate companionship of God.

To abandon the way of the world and follow the way of Jesus is a bold move and requires honest, careful, and prayerful consideration. It is not an inconsequential decision. Jesus himself told us to consider carefully the cost of discipleship: "For which of you, intending to build a tower, does not first sit down and estimate the cost, to see whether he has enough to complete it? . . . So therefore, none of you can become my disciple if you do not give up all your possessions" (Luke 14:28, 33 NRSV). . . .

To follow this Jesus is to desire to be like him in our living and our dying. (Job, *Three Simple Rules*, 27–28.)

Today, my God, I am asking you to bring back my heart from wherever it has wandered. My enthusiasm has waned. I feel like a dried-up brook. I reach for the hem of your garment. I can't find it. Yet even in this darkness you have prepared a feast. The feast is one of remembering the days of old when my brook was gushing with life.

The feast is a reminder that there will always be a bit of solid ground to stand on or wings to fly with. (Macrina Wiederkehr, *A Tree Full of Angels: Seeing the Holy in the Ordinary*, 150.)

We are chosen, blessed, and broken so as to be given. . . . For me, personally, this means that it is only as people who are given that we can fully understand our being chosen, blessed, and broken. In the giving it becomes clear that we are chosen, blessed, and broken not simply for our own sakes, but so that all we live finds its final significance in its being lived for others. (Henri J. M. Nouwen, *Life of the Beloved: Spiritual Living in a Secular World*, 84.)

True children of God realize in life's circumstances that we have no strength of our own. In all moments, we are to confess our weaknesses to do good by our own efforts. We know with St. Paul that all our strength is to be found in Christ. Our very weakness, when recognized, can become our strength as we lovingly surrender to God in all things. (Maloney, *In Jesus We Trust*, 134.)

Taking Time to Reflect

Pause and recall what you have read and heard, as well as your own life experiences. Take note of anything that particularly catches your attention—perhaps a word, phrase, or image.

Making Our Requests Known

Focus your prayers more specifically on particular things, persons, or circumstances. The following petitions offer guidance:

Prayers for God's Creation and Our World
Prayers for All God's People
Prayers for the Church and All Who Seek God
Prayers for Our Neighbors
Prayers for Our Families and Friends
Prayers for Ourselves

Thanking God for Our Prayers and Life

Loving God,
I offer open hands,
open mind, open heart,
and a willing spirit
to hear continually your calling
and sending voice.
I abandon my life
into your care
with the same assurance
that you will lead me
in paths of righteousness
and goodness. Amen.

Prayer at the End of the Day

Inviting God's Activity

Tender Shepherd of my soul, make yourself and your way known to me in this evening time of prayer and reflection. By the power of your presence, bring me to the end of the day whole, complete, and at peace with you, my neighbor, and myself. Grant a night of peaceful rest and send me forth tomorrow as a witness to your love and grace.

A Continuing Request

Create a clean heart for me, God;
>   put a new, faithful spirit deep inside me! (Psalm 51:10)

Gathering the Day

Remembering—Reflect on the day's experiences.

Confessing—Own up to your own weakness, failure, and sin.

Forgiving—Ask for and accept God's forgiveness, and forgive yourself and all who may have injured you or those you love.

Thanksgiving—Give thanks for the gifts that God has granted this day.

Offering

My whole being clings to you;
>   your strong hand upholds me. (Psalm 63:8)

Blessing

I will lie down and fall asleep in peace
>   because you alone, Lord, let me live in safety. (Psalm 4:8)

Week 18

Life Transformed

Approaching God with Intention

Loving God,
I bring myself into your presence
As I offer to you all that I am,
All that I hope to become,
For I am yours and I belong to you,
My faithful Savior and Guide.

 Sit in silence and stillness for a few moments, lengthening the time each day as you are able.

Becoming Aware of God's Presence

Tender Shepherd, who promised to be with us always,
    we welcome you now into our midst
        and invite you to stay with us all the day long.

Inviting God's Intervention

Come, tender Shepherd, and be our guide, strength,
    and companion in every experience of life today and always.

Listening for God's Voice

Open yourself to hear what God is saying to you through the Scriptures.

Some who were present on that occasion told Jesus about the Galileans whom Pilate had killed while they were offering sacrifices. He replied, "Do you think the suffering of these Galileans proves that they were more sinful than all the other Galileans? No, I tell you, but unless you change your hearts and lives, you will die just as they did. What about those eighteen people who were killed when the tower of Siloam fell on them? Do you think that they were more guilty of wrongdoing than everyone else who lives in Jerusalem? No, I tell you, but unless you change your hearts and lives, you will die just as they did."

Jesus told this parable: "A man owned a fig tree planted in his vineyard. He came looking for fruit on it and found none. He said to his gardener, 'Look, I've come looking for fruit on this fig tree for the past three years, and I've never found any. Cut it down! Why should it continue depleting the soil's nutrients?' The gardener responded, 'Lord, give it one more year, and I will dig around it and give it fertilizer. Maybe it will produce fruit next year; if not, then you can cut it down.'"

(Luke 13:1-9)

Alternative Readings

Romans 12:1-8

Psalm 51

Romans 12:14-21

Isaiah 55:1-9

Romans 13:8-14

Philippians 1:3-11

Practicing Spiritual Reading

As you read the essay and one or more quotations each day, do so with an openness for further contemplation on the week's theme. Ask God, Is there a word or prayer for my life in these words?

Living a transformed life does not happen by gritting our teeth and trying harder. It happens as we offer ourselves ever more fully to the One who knows us completely and loves us beyond our ability to comprehend. Of course, we are called to live a disciplined and faithful life, but not on our own. It is God who leads us, strengthens us, and sustains us in a life of faithfulness. And it is God who does the transforming work as we open ourselves more and more to the Spirit's presence, guidance, and grace. Paul's confession in 2 Corinthians 3:18 says it well: "And all of us, with unveiled faces, seeing the glory of the Lord as though reflected in a mirror, are being transformed into the same image from one degree of glory to another; for this comes from the Lord, the Spirit" (NRSV). When we spend our days and nights in God's presence, we too will reflect that divine image more and more. This is God's transforming work in progress in ordinary lives and ordinary times. May it always be the story of our lives.

 In prayer, we open ourselves to respond to God's presence and notice the light of God as it shines on the world, exposing fault yet also promising hope. We pay attention in a special way, focusing our yearning to be partners in God's reconciling love. We ask for God's help in saying yes to that which is life-giving in the deepest sense and in saying the specific no that will loosen whatever chains bind us and others to destruction. We thank God for life and love, and we beg God for mercy and strength, for ourselves and all creation. (Dorothy C. Bass and Craig Dykstra, "Practicing a Way of Life" in *Practicing Our Faith: A Way of Life for a Searching People*, 202.)

We cannot hope to follow God as revealed in Jesus if we never spend time together, allowing God to speak to us. On the other hand, the longer we intentionally live in God's presence—the longer we "hang out" with Jesus—the more like Jesus we become. The more we seek to remain in Christ's presence, the more the chalice of life that we have been given will be filled with divine presence, energy, wisdom, and direction. (Job, *Three Simple Questions*, 62–63.)

A long time ago, I heard Jean Houston tell a story about herself as a youth, going to hear a presentation by Helen Keller who was blind and deaf. Houston said that after Helen Keller finished speaking, she knew that she had to talk with her. She got up and presented her face to Helen Keller. Jean Houston described the experience this way: "She read my whole face and I blurted out: 'Miss Keller, why are you so happy?' and she laughed and laughed, saying: 'My child, it is because I live each day as if it were my last and life, with all its moments, is so full of glory.'" (Joyce Rupp, *The Cup of Our Life: A Guide to Spiritual Growth*, 145.)

Be bold enough to ask God to transform your own life and invest your life as leaven to transform the world where you are. Begin every day in seeking God's direction and companionship, and end every day in offering anew all you have done and all that you are to the One who gives you life. (Job, *A Wesleyan Spiritual Reader*, 194.)

Taking Time to Reflect

Pause and recall what you have read and heard, as well as your own life experiences. Take note of anything that particularly catches your attention—perhaps a word, phrase, or image.

Making Our Requests Known

Focus your prayers more specifically on particular things, persons, or circumstances. The following petitions offer guidance:

Prayers for God's Creation and Our World
Prayers for All God's People
Prayers for the Church and All Who Seek God
Prayers for Our Neighbors
Prayers for Our Families and Friends
Prayers for Ourselves

Thanking God for Our Prayers and Life

Grant to me, O God,
the continual guidance, strength,
and help of your Holy Spirit
so that I may serve faithfully
in your church and world.

Hear and accept my prayer
as I offer it and my life to you
in gratitude for your steadfast love.
In the name of Christ.
Amen.

Prayer at the End of the Day

Inviting God's Activity

Tender Shepherd of my soul, make yourself and your way known to me in this evening time of prayer and reflection. By the power of your presence, bring me to the end of the day whole, complete, and at peace with you, my neighbor, and myself. Grant a night of peaceful rest and send me forth tomorrow as a witness to your love and grace.

A Continuing Request

> Create a clean heart for me, God;
> put a new, faithful spirit deep inside me! (Psalm 51:10)

Gathering the Day

Remembering—Reflect on the day's experiences.

Confessing—Own up to your own weakness, failure, and sin.

Forgiving—Ask for and accept God's forgiveness, and forgive yourself and all who may have injured you or those you love.

Thanksgiving—Give thanks for the gifts that God has granted this day.

Offering

> My whole being clings to you;
> your strong hand upholds me. (Psalm 63:8)

Blessing

> I will lie down and fall asleep in peace
> because you alone, LORD, let me live in safety. (Psalm 4:8)

Week 19

Jesus Does the Unexpected

Approaching God with Intention

Faithful Savior,
Help me lay aside the burdens
and concerns of my life
long enough to hear your voice.
Lead me into the light of your truth
and prepare me for faithful and joyful discipleship.
Amen.

 Sit in silence and stillness for a few moments, lengthening the time each day as you are able.

Becoming Aware of God's Presence

> LORD, I have heard your reputation.
>> I have seen your work.
> Over time, revive it.
>> Over time, make it known.
> Though angry, remember compassion. (Habakkuk 3:2)

Inviting God's Intervention

> The LORD God is my strength.
>> He will set my feet like the deer.
>> He will let me walk upon the heights. (Habakkuk 3:19)

Listening for God's Voice

Open yourself to hear what God is saying to you through the Scriptures.

> Jesus went out beside the lake again. The whole crowd came to him, and he began to teach them. As he continued along, he saw Levi, Alphaeus' son, sitting at a kiosk for collecting taxes. Jesus said to him, "Follow me." Levi got up and followed him.
>
> Jesus sat down to eat at Levi's house. Many tax collectors and sinners were eating with Jesus and his disciples. Indeed, many of them had become his followers. When some of the legal experts from among the Pharisees saw that he was eating with sinners and tax collectors, they asked his disciples, "Why is he eating with sinners and tax collectors?"
>
> When Jesus heard it, he said to them, "Healthy people don't need a doctor, but sick people do. I didn't come to call righteous people, but sinners."
> (Mark 2:13-17)

Alternative Readings
Jeremiah 1:4-10
Matthew 20:1-16
Mark 12:13-17
2 Corinthians 5:16-21
Luke 17:1-19
Luke 22:24-37

Practicing Spiritual Reading

As you read the essay and one or more quotations each day, do so with an openness for further contemplation on the week's theme. Ask God, Is there a word or prayer for my life in these words?

Jesus often catches us off guard, and we are surprised by what he says and does. Just when we think we know Jesus really well, he surprises us and leaves us trying to catch our breath and catch up to where he is and where he is trying to lead us. The days leading up to his crucifixion and resurrection are no exception. Eugene H. Peterson, in the introduction to his book *Tell It Slant*, says, "As we listen in on Jesus as he talks and then participate with Jesus as he prays, I hope that together we, writer and readers, will develop a discerning aversion to all forms of depersonalizing godtalk that acquire a taste for and skills in the always personal language God uses, even in our conversations and small talk, maybe especially in our small talk, to make and save and bless us one and all" (p. 5). The chapters that follow make it clear that it was not just the language of Jesus that was clear and straightforward, but his actions as well. Jesus consistently did the unexpected, and he told stories about everyday events in unexpected ways to carry the truth of his out-of-the-ordinary message and life.

I have long been taken by the origin of the name "Christian." In Acts 11 there was a community of people who so lived out the Christ-life that they were called "Christians," which means "little Christs." . . . Here were people living a life that reflected the person of Jesus. . . . I think of the scandal of grace in the midst of community, the selflessness of compassion in the face of disdain, the aroma of holiness in the teeth of debauchery, the firmness of orthodoxy while immersed in the illusion of various matrices. But most of all, I suppose, I think of the scandal of grace—freely received into our lives and then freely distributed to others. Jesus himself said this should be the mark of the Christian, and the single dynamic that would arrest the world's attention. (Jim White quoted in David Kinnaman and Gabe Lyons, *Unchristian: What a New Generation Really Thinks about Christianity . . . and Why It Matters*, 237.)

In Jesus we see a God who does the unexpected and the unpredictable. We see Jesus choosing to be the friend of sinners and being just as comfortable with the very wealthy as he is with the homeless beggar. We see a God who refuses to accept the boundaries that culture establishes and who moves with ease among scholars, religious leaders, soldiers, prostitutes, farmers, fishermen, tax collectors, and demon-possessed men and women—inviting them all into a new way of seeing the world, a new way of living, a new kingdom. (Job, *Three Simple Questions*, 21.)

We need to become ever more sensitive to the call to prayer, be it external or inward. . . . From time to time, God's presence is felt within us, and we are invited to respond. Such incidents occur unpredictably and without preparation—in a pause between tasks, as a background to other activities or in a time of leisure. They may burst into consciousness, making it difficult to continue whatever we were doing. They may even arouse us from sleep. In an obscure and undefined way, we become aware that our whole self is being drawn toward God in a manner fundamentally independent of our conscious willing. (Casey, *Toward God*, 49.)

Taking Time to Reflection

Pause and recall what you have read and heard, as well as your own life experiences. Take note of anything that particularly catches your attention—perhaps a word, phrase, or image.

Making Our Requests Known

Focus your prayers more specifically on particular things, persons, or circumstances. The following petitions offer guidance:

Prayers for God's Creation and Our World
Prayers for All God's People
Prayers for the Church and All Who Seek God
Prayers for Our Neighbors
Prayers for Our Families and Friends
Prayers for Ourselves

Thanking God for Our Prayers and Life

Loving God,
Defend and uphold me
    and grant me grace
    to live in such a way as to please you
    and reflect your presence to others.
Hear and accept my prayer
    as I offer it and my life to you
    in gratitude for your steadfast love.
In the name of Christ. Amen.

Prayer at the End of the Day

Inviting God's Activity

Tender Shepherd of my soul, make yourself and your way known to me in this evening time of prayer and reflection. By the power of your presence, bring me to the end of the day whole, complete, and at peace with you, my neighbor, and myself. Grant a night of peaceful rest and send me forth tomorrow as a witness to your love and grace.

A Continuing Request

> Create a clean heart for me, God;
> > put a new, faithful spirit deep inside me! (Psalm 51:10)

Gathering the Day

Remembering—Reflect on the day's experiences.

Confessing—Own up to your own weakness, failure, and sin.

Forgiving—Ask for and accept God's forgiveness, and forgive yourself and all who may have injured you or those you love.

Thanksgiving—Give thanks for the gifts that God has granted this day.

Offering

> My whole being clings to you;
> > your strong hand upholds me. (Psalm 63:8)

Blessing

> I will lie down and fall asleep in peace
> > because you alone, Lord, let me live in safety. (Psalm 4:8)

Week 20

Hope: Promise and Fulfillment

Approaching God with Intention

Make your ways known to me, LORD;
>   teach me your paths.
Lead me in your truth—teach it to me—
>   because you are the God who saves me.
>   I put my hope in you all day long.
LORD, remember your compassion and faithful love—
>   they are forever! (Psalm 25:4-6)

 Sit in silence and stillness for a few moments, lengthening the time each day as you are able.

Becoming Aware of God's Presence

Let your acts be seen by your servants;
>   let your glory be seen by their children. (Psalm 90:16)

Inviting God's Intervention

Fill us full every morning with your faithful love
>   so we can rejoice and celebrate our whole life long.
>   (Psalm 90:14)

Listening for God's Voice

Open yourself to hear what God is saying to you through the Scriptures.

> May the God and Father of our Lord Jesus Christ be blessed!
> On account of his vast mercy, he has given us new birth. You
> have been born anew into a living hope through the resurrection
> of Jesus Christ from the dead. You have a pure and enduring
> inheritance that cannot perish—an inheritance that is presently
> kept safe in heaven for you. Through his faithfulness, you are
> guarded by God's power so that you can receive the salvation he is
> ready to reveal in the last time.

Alternative Readings

Genesis 9:1-17
Ephesians 1:15-23
Jeremiah 31:31-34
Psalm 130
1 Peter 1:13-21
Ephesians 2:11-22

> You now rejoice in this hope, even if it's necessary
> for you to be distressed for a short time by various
> trials. This is necessary so that your faith may
> be found genuine. (Your faith is more valuable
> than gold, which will be destroyed even though
> it is itself tested by fire.) Your genuine faith will
> result in praise, glory, and honor for you when
> Jesus Christ is revealed. Although you've never
> seen him, you love him. Even though you don't
> see him now, you trust him and so rejoice with a
> glorious joy that is too much for words. You are receiving the goal
> of your faith: your salvation. (1 Peter 1:3-9)

Practicing Spiritual Reading

As you read the essay and one or more quotations each day, do so with an openness for further contemplation on the week's theme. Ask God, Is there a word or prayer for my life in these words?

My hopes are often so timid and tame that I hardly notice when they don't come to pass. So it did rain when I was going to mow the lawn. Small matter. Not at all like the hope about which our Scriptures speak this week. Here is hope at the very center of life. It is hope that is the promise of earthshaking and life-changing magnitude. You and I are children of God who are promised our full inheritance as God's beloved. Why should we fear? The living God has promised to be our companion in every experience of life, in this world and the next. No one can separate us from God or from our inheritance as a child of God. It is ours and by God's grace we may claim it now. Paul put it this way, "I pray that the God of our Lord Jesus Christ, the Father of glory, may give you a spirit of wisdom and revelation as you come to know him, so that, with the eyes of your heart enlightened, you may know what is the hope to which he has called you, what are the riches of his glorious inheritance among the saints . . ." (Ephesians 1:17-18 NRSV).

Hope for wild, wonderful, and too-good-to-be-true results such as actual signs of God's kingdom sprouting up all over the world, in your community, and even in your life. And then let your life and your prayer reflect that hope this day and always. Your kingdom come on earth as it is in heaven.

It has been said that Charles Wesley's hymns always begin on earth and end in heaven. So it is with John Wesley's theology. He was firmly convinced of the coming day of Christ, which is not yet, but toward which humankind, with the whole creation, is moving. . . . John Wesley had a doctrine of final things, an eschatology, in which God's kingdom is being presently realized even as it points toward a consummating future. The Christian lives with the lively hope that God, who has begun a good thing, will fulfill it in the day of Jesus Christ. (Thomas A. Langford, *Practical Divinity: Theology in the Wesleyan Tradition*, Vol. 1, 36-37.)

God is sovereign and therefore God is able to care for and provide for all of creation.

In a world of almost instant communication and graphic story-telling about the tragedy and pain of the world, it is easy to forget this ancient truth.

Once we lose the concept of God as sovereign, our prayers, our faith, and our very souls begin to shrink. . . .

Commitment to a god that is too small will stifle any hope for a transformed world and dull our efforts to bring such a world into being. (Job, *A Wesleyan Spiritual Reader*, 43.)

The Prayer of Relinquishment is a bona fide letting go, but it is a release with hope. We have no fatalist resignation. We are buoyed up by a confident trust in the character of God. Even when all we see are tangled threads on the backside of life's tapestry, we know that God is good and is out to do us good always. That gives us hope to believe that we are the winners, regardless of what we are being called upon to relinquish. (Foster, *Prayer*, 52.)

"Anyone who follows me shall not walk in darkness," says the Lord. These are the words of Christ, and by them we are reminded that we must imitate his life and his ways if we are to be truly enlightened and set free from the darkness of our own hearts. Let it be the most important thing we do, then, to reflect on the life of Jesus Christ. (Thomas à Kempis, *The Imitation of Christ*, 30.)

Taking Time to Reflect

Pause and recall what you have read and heard, as well as your own life experiences. Take note of anything that particularly catches your attention—perhaps a word, phrase, or image.

Making Our Requests Known

Focus your prayers more specifically on particular things, persons, or circumstances. The following petitions offer guidance:

Prayers for God's Creation and Our World
Prayers for All God's People
Prayers for the Church and All Who Seek God
Prayers for Our Neighbors
Prayers for Our Families and Friends
Prayers for Ourselves

Thanking God for Our Prayers and Life

I offer my life to you, Lord.
> My God, I trust you.
Please don't let me be put to shame!
> Don't let my enemies rejoice over me!
For that matter,
> don't let anyone who hopes in you
> > be put to shame;
instead, let those who are treacherous without excuse be put to shame. (Psalm 25:1-3)

Prayer at the End of the Day

Inviting God's Activity

Tender Shepherd of my soul, make yourself and your way known to me in this evening time of prayer and reflection. By the power of your presence, bring me to the end of the day whole, complete, and at peace with you, my neighbor, and myself. Grant a night of peaceful rest and send me forth tomorrow as a witness to your love and grace.

A Continuing Request

Create a clean heart for me, God;
>> put a new, faithful spirit deep inside me! (Psalm 51:10)

Gathering the Day

Remembering—Reflect on the day's experiences.

Confessing—Own up to your own weakness, failure, and sin.

Forgiving—Ask for and accept God's forgiveness, and forgive yourself and all who may have injured you or those you love.

Thanksgiving—Give thanks for the gifts that God has granted this day.

Offering

My whole being clings to you;
>> your strong hand upholds me. (Psalm 63:8)

Blessing

I will lie down and fall asleep in peace
>> because you alone, Lord, let me live in safety. (Psalm 4:8)

Week 21

Truth on Trial

Approaching God with Intention

God revealed in so many ways
The beauty and magnificence of creation
The words of prophet, priest, and servant
The life, death, resurrection of Jesus
The power and constant presence of your Spirit
I bring myself into your presence
As I offer to you all that I am
All that I hope to become
My faithful Savior and Guide.

 *Sit in silence and stillness for a few moments, lengthening the time
each day as you are able.*

Becoming Aware of God's Presence

I've taken refuge in you, LORD.
    Don't let me ever be put to shame!
Deliver me and rescue me by your righteousness!
    Bend your ear toward me and save me!
Be my rock of refuge
    where I can always escape.

You commanded that my life be saved
>because you are my rock and my fortress. (Psalm 71:1-3)

Inviting God's Intervention

My God, rescue me from the power of the wicked;
>rescue me from the grip of the wrongdoer and the oppressor.
>>(Psalm 71:4)

Listening for God's Voice

Open yourself to hear what God is saying to you through the Scriptures.

The whole assembly got up and led Jesus to Pilate and began to accuse him. They said, "We have found this man misleading our people, opposing the payment of taxes to Caesar, and claiming that he is the Christ, a king."

Pilate asked him, "Are you the king of the Jews?"

Jesus replied, "That's what you say."

Then Pilate said to the chief priests and the crowds, "I find no legal basis for action against this man."

But they objected strenuously, saying, "He agitates the people with his teaching throughout Judea—starting from Galilee all the way here."

Hearing this, Pilate asked if the man was a Galilean. When he learned that Jesus was from Herod's district, Pilate sent him to Herod, who was also in Jerusalem at that time. Herod was very glad to see Jesus, for he had heard about Jesus and had wanted to see him for quite some time. He was hoping to see Jesus perform some sign. Herod questioned Jesus at length, but Jesus didn't respond to him. The chief priests and

Alternative Readings

Psalm 71:12-18
John 13:21-30
Hebrews 12:1-3
Psalm 31:9-16
1 Corinthians 1:18-25
1 Peter 4:12-19

the legal experts were there, fiercely accusing Jesus. Herod and his soldiers treated Jesus with contempt. Herod mocked him by dressing Jesus in elegant clothes and sent him back to Pilate. Pilate and Herod became friends with each other that day. Before this, they had been enemies. (Luke 23:1-12)

Practicing Spiritual Reading

As you read the essay and one or more quotations each day, do so with an openness for further contemplation on the week's theme. Ask God, Is there a word or prayer for my life in these words?

Jesus got into a lot of trouble in his brief ministry, and it was always for all the right reasons. His message was radical and dangerous to the ears of religious and political leaders. However, this same message was wonderful, redeeming truth to the average, the poor, and the oppressed persons of his time. Some of this week's Scripture readings give us a glimpse of his final days leading to his trial and crucifixion. Jesus said, "Whoever has seen me has seen the Father" (John 14:9 NRSV). And the writer of Colossians says, "He is the image of the invisible God" (1:15 NRSV). It is clear from the Scripture record that the reality of truth, righteousness, and goodness were on trial with Jesus as he begins his week as the prince of peace and ends it as an executed criminal. It may seem as though truth, goodness, righteousness, and God have lost it all in this one week of confrontation. Fortunately, it is not the end of the story. In the meantime, we ask ourselves, "How are we doing in telling the truth about goodness, righteousness, Jesus, and God?"

Jesus chose the way of peace in a violent world. He taught his disciples to do the same. Just for a moment Peter forgot, and because of that, one of the arresting party lost an ear. But still Jesus rebuked Peter and courageously continued his journey as the Prince of Peace on the way to his own death. (Norman Shawchuck and Rueben P. Job, *A Guide to Prayer for All Who Seek God*, 164.)

I do see the future Christian faith being something that is good, true, and credible in our culture. I can dream of a day when the followers of Jesus are known not for these current tragic perceptions, but for trying to live like Jesus. We will fumble, stumble, and hit some rough patches along the way, but we must not give up. . . . Christians will be the first to sound the cry of injustice and rally the nations that we all must do more. (Mike Foster quoted in Kinnaman and Lyons, *Unchristian*, 242–243.)

It is encouraging to remember that prayer is not all up to us. God is always pursuing us, always trying to get our attention, always seeking relationship with us. Best of all, as Paul declares, the Holy Spirit assists us every step of the way: "We don't know what we should pray, but the Spirit himself pleads our case" (Romans 8:26).

If you have the desire to pray, you already have everything it takes to live a life of prayer. Permit the Spirit to guide you as you pray and as you journey deeper into a life of prayer. (Job, *Listen*, 52.)

The work of following Christ is like working with a psychotherapist who has a clear insight into what is wrong with us. With incredible accuracy, God puts his finger on exactly the spot that needs attention at this precise time in our spiritual growth. If we are hanging on to one last shred of possessiveness, he comes along and says, often through some person or event, "Won't you give this to me?" (Thomas Keating, *Invitation to Love: The Way of Christian Contemplation*, 18.)

Taking Time to Reflect

 Pause and recall what you have read and heard, as well as your own life experiences. Take note of anything that particularly catches your attention—perhaps a word, phrase, or image.

Making Our Requests Known

Focus your prayers more specifically on particular things, persons, or circumstances. The following petitions offer guidance:

Prayers for God's Creation and Our World
Prayers for All God's People
Prayers for the Church and All Who Seek God

Prayers for Our Neighbors
Prayers for Our Families and Friends
Prayers for Ourselves

Thanking God for Our Prayers and Life

> Your faithfulness extends from one generation to the next!
> > You set the earth firmly in place, and it is still there.
> Your rules endure to this day
> > because everything serves you.
> If your Instruction hadn't been my delight,
> > I would have died because of my suffering.
> I will never forget your precepts
> > because through them you gave me life again.
> I'm yours—save me
> > because I've pursued your precepts! (Psalm 119:90-94)

Prayer at the End of the Day

Inviting God's Activity

Tender Shepherd of my soul, make yourself and your way known to me in this evening time of prayer and reflection. By the power of your presence, bring me to the end of the day whole, complete, and at peace with you, my neighbor, and myself. Grant a night of peaceful rest and send me forth tomorrow as a witness to your love and grace.

A Continuing Request

> Create a clean heart for me, God;
>> put a new, faithful spirit deep inside me! (Psalm 51:10)

Gathering the Day

Remembering—Reflect on the day's experiences.

Confessing—Own up to your own weakness, failure, and sin.

Forgiving—Ask for and accept God's forgiveness, and forgive yourself and all who may have injured you or those you love.

Thanksgiving—Give thanks for the gifts that God has granted this day.

Offering

> My whole being clings to you;
>> your strong hand upholds me. (Psalm 63:8)

Blessing

> I will lie down and fall asleep in peace
>> because you alone, Lord, let me live in safety. (Psalm 4:8)

Week 22

Jesus Goes on Ahead

Approaching God with Intention

Faithful Savior,
deliver me from the false impression
that I can follow you,
love as you did,
and live as you did
on my own strength.
Help me honestly examine my life
in the light of your presence this day.
Lead me beyond self-examination
and confession
to forgiveness and new life.
Amen.

 Sit in silence and stillness for a few moments, lengthening the time each day as you are able.

Becoming Aware of God's Presence

> While they were discussing these things, Jesus himself arrived and joined them on their journey. (Luke 24:15)

Inviting God's Intervention

But they urged him, saying, "Stay with us. It's nearly evening, and the day is almost over." So he went in to stay with them.

(Luke 24:29)

Listening for God's Voice

Open yourself to hear what God is saying to you through the Scriptures.

When the Sabbath was over, Mary Magdalene, Mary the mother of James, and Salome bought spices so that they could go and anoint Jesus' dead body. Very early on the first day of the week, just after sunrise, they came to the tomb. They were saying to each other, "Who's going to roll the stone away from the entrance for us?" When they looked up, they saw that the stone had been rolled away. (And it was a very large stone!) Going into the tomb, they saw a young man in a white robe seated on the right side; and they were startled. But he said to them, "Don't be alarmed! You are looking for Jesus of Nazareth, who was crucified. He has been raised. He isn't here. Look, here's the place where they laid him. Go, tell his disciples, especially Peter, that he is going ahead of you into Galilee. You will see him there, just as he told you." Overcome with terror and dread, they fled from the tomb. They said nothing to anyone, because they were afraid. (Mark 16:1-8)

Alternative Readings

Matthew 28:1-10
Isaiah 25:1-9
John 14:1-14
Acts 4:1-12
Psalm 118:1-2, 14-24
1 Corinthians 15:1-11

Practicing Spiritual Reading

As you read the essay and one or more quotations each day, do so with an openness for further contemplation on the week's theme. Ask God, Is there a word or prayer for my life in these words?

It was a great comfort for me to have my father on ahead with his plow and five horses creating an arrow-straight, half-mile-long furrow. I followed along with my smaller plow and three horses confident that if I simply kept one wheel of the plow in the furrow I would leave that arrow-straight furrow behind me as well. It was a comfort to have him on ahead because he knew where the rocky and muddy areas were and when to lift the plow to preserve the grassed-over waterways.

There was one other reason I wanted to stay close to him. I couldn't have explained it then. But now, in my eight decades of life, I know it was the desire for his company that kept me close. Even then, young boys had their own questions of self-worth, their own feelings of loneliness, and their own anxiety about tomorrow. But in the company of my father, the one whose love had never failed or forsaken me, all was well. Neither cold nor rain could drive me away. For even then I knew all was well in the company of the one who seemed to know how to do everything and who loved me so deeply. Jesus spoke to the women visiting the tomb, "Do not be afraid; go and tell my brothers to go to Galilee; there they will see me" (Matthew 28:10 NRSV). Who are you following into the future?

Prayer is our means of taking a sighting, of re-orienting ourselves—by re-establishing contact with our goal. In the presence of God many components of our life fall into perspective and our journey begins to make more sense. We look toward God, conscious that seeking what is unseen corresponds to a very deep stratum of our being. It is not just a bright idea or a fad; it grows from the soil of the heart. Prayer is inseparable from living. (Casey, *Toward God*, 5.)

This kind of blessing prayer is called a benediction. It comes at the end of something, to send people on their way. All I am saying is that anyone can do this. Anyone can ask and anyone can bless, whether anyone has authorized you to do it or not. . . . That we are able to bless one another at all is evidence that we have been blessed, whether we can remember when or not. That we are willing to bless one another is miracle enough to stagger the very stars. (Barbara Brown Taylor, *An Altar in the World: A Geography of Faith*, 208–209.)

In Jesus we see a God who is never under our control but always free of any control, and who may act and create as it seems wise and is in keeping with God's will.

Jesus reveals a God who is always and forever beyond us, completely other than we are, and yet who wants to come and dwell within us (John 14:23). Jesus reveals a God of love. (Job, *Three Simple Questions*, 22.)

Taking Time to Reflect

 Pause and recall what you have read and heard, as well as your own life experiences. Take note of anything that particularly catches your attention—perhaps a word, phrase, or image.

Making Our Requests Known

Focus your prayers more specifically on particular things, persons, or circumstances. The following petitions offer guidance:

Prayers for God's Creation and Our World
Prayers for All God's People
Prayers for the Church and All Who Seek God
Prayers for Our Neighbors
Prayers for Our Families and Friends
Prayers for Ourselves

Thanking God for Our Prayers and Life

Bless the LORD
    because he has listened to my request for mercy!
The LORD is my strength and my shield.
    My heart trusts him.
        I was helped, my heart rejoiced,
            and I thank him with my song. (Psalm 28:6-7)

Prayer at the End of the Day

Inviting God's Activity

Tender Shepherd of my soul, make yourself and your way known to me in this evening time of prayer and reflection. By the power of your presence, bring me to the end of the day whole, complete, and at peace with you, my neighbor, and myself. Grant a night of peaceful rest and send me forth tomorrow as a witness to your love and grace.

A Continuing Request

Create a clean heart for me, God;
    put a new, faithful spirit deep inside me! (Psalm 51:10)

Gathering the Day

Remembering—Reflect on the day's experiences.

Confessing—Own up to your own weakness, failure, and sin.

Forgiving—Ask for and accept God's forgiveness, and forgive yourself and all who may have injured you or those you love.

Thanksgiving—Give thanks for the gifts that God has granted this day.

Offering

My whole being clings to you;
    your strong hand upholds me. (Psalm 63:8)

Blessing

I will lie down and fall asleep in peace
    because you alone, LORD, let me live in safety. (Psalm 4:8)

Prayer Practice

Remembering Who You Are

Whenever he was troubled or dismayed, the reformer
Martin Luther would remember his baptism. . . .
Remembering his baptism reassured Luther
that he was a beloved child of God, that no threat
could frighten him, and that no power could snatch
him from the loving arms of God.

Those familiar with Luther's custom have found a practice
of their own to remind themselves who they are, and it is
something that can be practiced by all Christians.
The practice is simply to speak your own name, put your
fingers to your head, and repeat, "Remember who you
are." As you do this, remember your baptism and affirm
that you are a beloved child of God. Then offer a prayer
of thanks. This simple practice can be a reassuring
reminder of who we are as children of God.
(Job, *Three Simple Questions*, 48.)

Week 23

You Can Trust Me

Approaching God with Intention

Loving God,
I offer open hands, open mind, open heart,
and a willing spirit
to hear continually your calling and sending voice.
I abandon my life into your care
with the assurance that you will lead me
in paths of righteousness and goodness.
Amen.

 Sit in silence and stillness for a few moments, lengthening the time each day if you are able.

Becoming Aware of God's Presence

My heart is unwavering, God.
I will sing and make music—
    yes, with my whole being! . . .
    because your faithful love is higher than heaven;
    your faithfulness reaches the clouds. (Psalm 108:1, 4)

Inviting God's Intervention

> Give justice to the lowly and the orphan;
>> maintain the right of the poor and the destitute!
> Rescue the lowly and the needy.
>> Deliver them from the power of the wicked! (Psalm 82:3-4)

Listening for God's Voice

Open yourself to hear what God is saying to you through the Scriptures.

John, to the seven churches that are in Asia:

Grace and peace to you from the one who is and was and is coming, and from the seven spirits that are before God's throne, and from Jesus Christ—the faithful witness, the firstborn from among the dead, and the ruler of the kings of the earth.

To the one who loves us and freed us from our sins by his blood, who made us a kingdom, priests to his God and Father—to him be glory and power forever and always. Amen.

Look, he is coming with the clouds! Every eye will see him, including those who pierced him, and all the tribes of the earth will mourn because of him. This is so. Amen. "I am the Alpha and the Omega," says the Lord God, "the one who is and was and is coming, the Almighty."

(Revelation 1:4-8)

Alternative Readings

John 20:19-31
Hebrews 2:1-13
John 4:39-45
Psalm 28:6-9
1 John 5:1-5
Psalm 16

Practicing Spiritual Reading

As you read the essay and one or more quotations each day, do so with an openness for further contemplation on the week's theme. Ask God, Is there a word or prayer for my life in these words?

Thomas wanted to see for himself. Paul when giving witness to the church at Corinth used his own experience of the living Christ as proof of the reality of the Resurrection. We can understand the desire for that once-and-for-all physical proof that Jesus is alive and in our midst. When our dreams are cruelly crushed, as were those that Thomas had, we too begin to wonder, can we really trust Jesus and his promise to never forsake us? Or, are we on our own? Two thousand years of history tell us, "Yes, we can trust him," and, "No, we are never alone." God has granted the gift of long life to me, and while I have never put my hands in the wounds of Jesus, I am more confident than ever that God is with me and that the testimony of the early church is trustworthy. "I am convinced that neither death, nor life, nor angels, nor rulers, nor things present, nor things to come, nor powers, nor height, nor depth, nor anything else in all creation, will be able to separate us from the love of God in Christ Jesus our Lord" (Romans 8:38-39 NRSV). This is enough for me. How about you?

 By the loving power of God, Jesus is transformed into glory, he is raised up. Such existence is beyond our imagination, for it is life in another dimension beyond the limits of time and space; it is life in the dimension of God. . . . Rather than coming to nothing in death, Jesus died into God. He is risen, whole and entire, as the embodied person he was in this life—his wounds are a sign of that. (Johnson, *Consider Jesus*, 59–60.)

The gist of the post-resurrectional message of Jesus to his disciples has been summed up in the words, "Peace! I am alive. There is work for you to do." This message points not only to the ground of intercessory prayer but to the re-enlistment the full resources of the one who prays into the labor force of the kingdom of God. Indeed there is work for you to do and real prayer seldom concludes without some intimation of a work assignment. For if prayer in one sense is a disengagement—a stepping aside from life in order to look at it in the deepest perspective, to see it under the gaze of God—it does not stop there. (Douglas V. Steere, *Dimensions of Prayer*, 95.)

In his sonnet "The Resurrection," John Dunne wrote, "He was all gold when he lay down, but rose / All tincture." Donne was referring to alchemy, whose ultimate object was not just to turn baser metals into gold, but to discover a tincture that would turn any metal it touched into gold. The risen Christ had become this tincture, turning the lives he touched into "gold." Thenceforth, his people would be Jesus' body, doing what he would do if he still had physical hands and feet. (Huston Smith, *The Soul of Christianity: Restoring the Great Tradition*, 74–75.)

Taking Time to Reflect

 Pause and recall what you have read and heard, as well as your own life experiences. Take note of anything that particularly catches your attention—perhaps a word, phrase, or image.

Making Our Requests Known

Focus your prayers more specifically on particular things, persons, or circumstances. The following petitions offer guidance:

Prayers for God's Creation and Our World
Prayers for All God's People
Prayers for the Church and All Who Seek God
Prayers for Our Neighbors
Prayers for Our Families and Friends
Prayers for Ourselves

Thanking God for Our Prayers and Life

God,
Greater than anything I can imagine,
I tremble in awe of such greatness and love;
I fall on my knees in gratitude and humility;
I yield my will to yours;
I declare that I am yours alone
    and invite you to do with me what you will
As I walk in the light and life
    of your unfailing presence.

Prayer at the End of the Day

Inviting God's Activity

Tender Shepherd of my soul, make yourself and your way known to me in this evening time of prayer and reflection. By the power of your presence, bring me to the end of the day whole, complete, and at peace with you, my neighbor, and myself. Grant a night of peaceful rest and send me forth tomorrow as a witness to your love and grace.

A Continuing Request

Create a clean heart for me, God;
>   put a new, faithful spirit deep inside me! (Psalm 51:10)

Gathering the Day

Remembering—Reflect on the day's experiences.

Confessing —Own up to your own weakness, failure, and sin.

Forgiving—Ask for and accept God's forgiveness, and forgive yourself and all who may have injured you or those you love.

Thanksgiving—Give thanks for the gifts that God has granted this day.

Offering

My whole being clings to you;
>   your strong hand upholds me. (Psalm 63:8)

Blessing

I will lie down and fall asleep in peace
>   because you alone, LORD, let me live in safety. (Psalm 4:8)

Week 24

When Faith Overcomes Fear

Approaching God with Intention

Faithful Savior,
who became one of us to make your way
and your Self known to humankind,
reveal your way and your Presence to me.
Help me lay aside the burdens and concerns of my life
long enough to hear your voice.
Amen.

 Sit in silence and stillness for a few moments, lengthening the time each day if you are able.

Becoming Aware of God's Presence

I've considered my ways and turned my feet back to your laws.
I hurry to keep your commandments—
    I never put it off! (Psalm 119:59-60)

Inviting God's Intervention

Your hands have made me and set me in place.
    Help me understand so I can learn your commandments.
                                                    (Psalm 119:73)

Listening for God's Voice

Open yourself to hear what God is saying to you through the Scriptures.

"Disciples aren't greater than their teacher, and slaves aren't greater than their master. It's enough for disciples to be like their teacher and slaves like their master. If they have called the head of the house Beelzebul, it's certain that they will call the members of his household by even worse names.

"Therefore, don't be afraid of those people because nothing is hidden that won't be revealed, and nothing secret that won't be brought out into the open. What I say to you in the darkness, tell in the light; and what you hear whispered, announce from the rooftops. Don't be afraid of those who kill the body but can't kill the soul. Instead, be afraid of the one who can destroy both body and soul in hell. Aren't two sparrows sold for a small coin? But not one of them will fall to the ground without your Father knowing about it already. Even the hairs of your head are all counted. Don't be afraid. You are worth more than many sparrows. (Matthew 10:24-31)

Alternative Readings
Luke 12:32-34
Philippians 1:12-18
Psalm 30
1 Peter 3:8-22
John 14:23-31
1 Thessalonians 1

Practicing Spiritual Reading

As you read the essay and one or more quotations each day, do so with an openness for further contemplation on the week's theme. Ask God, Is there a word or prayer for my life in these words?

With dreams dashed and hopes riddled by fear, the followers of Jesus sought to make sense of the past and chart a new course for the future. The sights and sounds of the public execution of their leader were impossible to forget, and the danger did not go away. As their numbers grew so did the dangers that stalked them day and night. It is not surprising that sometimes fear kept them behind closed doors. What is surprising is that their faith conquered their fear and transformed them into confident, bold, and effective witnesses to the life, death, resurrection, and message of Jesus. Their words and their lives were in harmony with the gospel, and this new movement quickly attracted large numbers of followers.

There are still places today where the danger of persecution stalks the followers of Christ and fear is an ever-present reality. For most of us, our fears are of a different nature but are no less real. It was faith in the presence of Jesus in their midst and on their journey that overcame fear in those early disciples. It is still the perfect response to fear today. Let's remind each other and ourselves every day this week that Jesus is in our midst and walks with each of us in our journey of life. Thanks be to God!

Life in Christ brings great gifts that so many times are left unclaimed by those of us who start the Christian journey but are quick to turn away from the fullness of life that is offered. Our inheritance of assurance, comfort, and peace, life abundant and eternal is often not incorporated into our daily life. Because it is not, we live anxious, fearful and incomplete lives, and we begin to wonder what difference our faith really makes. Life in Christ changes all of that as we live in the presence and power of Jesus Christ. (Job, *A Wesleyan Spiritual Reader*, 37.)

The early Christians adopted the initiation rite of baptism. Unlike the gender-specific Jewish ritual of circumcision, open only to males, baptism is inclusive since it is administered the same way to persons of both genders. Indicative of this, Paul's letter to the Galatians contains an early Christian baptismal hymn. As the newly baptized come up out of the water, all in white, wet robes, they sing, "Now there is no more Jew or Greek, slave or free, male or female, but all are one in Christ Jesus" (3:28). All divisions based on race, or class, or even gender are transcended in the oneness of the body of Christ. The power of the risen Christ becomes effective to the extent that this vision becomes reality in the community. (Johnson, *Consider Jesus*, 111.)

Our world may tremble, shake, and even collapse, but God will not collapse and will never let you go. You can never walk out of or fall out of God's incredible love for you. The disciples found comfort in this truth and so should we. Every moment of our existence, no matter where we are and no matter what our condition, we are bathed in God's amazing grace and love. (Job, *Life Stories*, 67.)

Taking Time to Reflect

 Pause and recall what you have read and heard, as well as your own life experiences. Take note of anything that particularly catches your attention—perhaps a word, phrase, or image.

Making Our Requests Known

Focus your prayers more specifically on particular things, persons, or circumstances. The following petitions offer guidance:

Prayers for God's Creation and Our World
Prayers for All God's People
Prayers for the Church and All Who Seek God
Prayers for Our Neighbors
Prayers for Our Families and Friends
Prayers for Ourselves

Thanking God for Our Prayers and Life

The LORD is my shepherd.
    I lack nothing.
He lets me rest in grassy meadows;
    he leads me to restful waters;
        he keeps me alive.
He guides me in proper paths
    for the sake of his good name.
Even when I walk through the darkest valley,
    I fear no danger because you are with me. . . .

Yes, goodness and faithful love
    will pursue me all the days of my life,
    and I will live in the LORD's house
    as long as I live. (Psalm 23:1-4a, 6)

Prayer at the End of the Day

Inviting God's Activity

Tender Shepherd of my soul, make yourself and your way known to me in this evening time of prayer and reflection. By the power of your presence, bring me to the end of the day whole, complete, and at peace with you, my neighbor, and myself. Grant a night of peaceful rest and send me forth tomorrow as a witness to your love and grace.

A Continuing Request

Create a clean heart for me, God;
> put a new, faithful spirit deep inside me! (Psalm 51:10)

Gathering the Day

Remembering—Reflect on the day's experiences.

Confessing—Own up to your own weakness, failure, and sin.

Forgiving—Ask for and accept God's forgiveness, and forgive yourself and all who may have injured you or those you love.

Thanksgiving—Give thanks for the gifts that God has granted this day.

Offering

My whole being clings to you;
> your strong hand upholds me. (Psalm 63:8)

Blessing

I will lie down and fall asleep in peace
> because you alone, LORD, let me live in safety. (Psalm 4:8)

Week 25

The Good Shepherd

Approaching God with Intention

Tender Shepherd,
guide me through the hours of this day.
Bring to my awareness your constant companionship,
to my weariness your matchless strength,
to my brokenness your healing touch,
and to my joy your blessing.
Amen.

 Sit in silence and stillness for a few moments, lengthening the time each day if you are able.

Becoming Aware of God's Presence

The LORD is my shepherd.
    I lack nothing. (Psalm 23:1)

Inviting God's Intervention

Make your ways known to me, LORD;
    teach me your paths.
Lead me in your truth—teach it to me—
    because you are the God who saves me.
        I put my hope in you all day long. (Psalm 25:4-5)

Listening for God's Voice

Open yourself to hear what God is saying to you through the Scriptures.

"I am the good shepherd. The good shepherd lays down his life for the sheep. When the hired hand sees the wolf coming, he leaves the sheep and runs away. That's because he isn't the shepherd; the sheep aren't really his. So the wolf attacks the sheep and scatters them. He's only a hired hand and the sheep don't matter to him.

"I am the good shepherd. I know my own sheep and they know me, just as the Father knows me and I know the Father. I give up my life for the sheep. I have other sheep that don't belong to this sheep pen. I must lead them too. They will listen to my voice and there will be one flock, with one shepherd.

"This is why the Father loves me: I give up my life so that I can take it up again. No one takes it from me, but I give it up because I want to. I have the right to give it up, and I have the right to take it up again. I received this commandment from my Father."

(John 10:11-18)

Alternative Readings

Isaiah 40:6-11
Ezekiel 34:11-16
Matthew 9:35-38
Psalm 23
Ezekiel 34:25-31
Luke 13:22-30

Practicing Spiritual Reading

As you read the essay and one or more quotations each day, do so with an openness for further contemplation on the week's theme. Ask God, Is there a word or prayer for my life in these words?

The late winter storm came up quickly with high winds that forced the heavy snow into large drifts and made movement of our small flock of sheep almost impossible. At the first sign of the storm, my father took his three sons to gather up the sheep and put them into a dry barn with straw for bedding and hay we carried in for them to eat. We had a large number of cattle on our farm but only a few sheep to complete a 4-H project for my two older brothers and me. The goal was to learn all about raising sheep so that they could be a profitable part of our diversified farm. We had already learned that they were gentle and lovable animals and that they had a tendency to nibble their way into trouble. Now we learned another of their weaknesses in the midst of a late winter North Dakota snowstorm.

Jesus describes himself as "the good shepherd" who knows and understands the ways of every sheep and will lay down his life for their well-being. For me it is a strong image of God's knowledge of each of us and of God's love and care for each of us. The Gospel readings from John and the Twenty-third Psalm continue to be a great source of comfort, security, and hope for me as I learn to trust and follow the Good Shepherd. Where do you find your comfort, security, and hope today?

The notion of unmerited mercy is quaint but unintelligible to most of us, since it has no prototype in our human experience. The dramatic surprise that comes in the stories of the searching shepherd, the searching woman, and the searching father is that being found by a searching God is more important than anything we do. If the message fails to resonate within us, we can't fault the messenger. (Brennan Manning, *The Wisdom of Tenderness: What Happens When God's Fierce Mercy Transforms Our Lives*, 138.)

The House of God stretches from one corner of the universe to the other. Sea monsters and ostriches live in it, along with people who pray in languages I do not speak, whose names I will never know. I am not in charge of this House, and never will be. I have no say about who is in and who is out. I do not get to make the rules. . . . I am a guest here, charged with serving other guests—even those who present themselves as my enemies. (Taylor, *An Altar in the World*, 13–14.)

We may name our spiritual disciplines differently, but we too must find our way of living and practicing those disciplines that will keep us in love with God—practices that will help keep us positioned in such a way that we may hear and be responsive to God's slightest whisper of direction. . . .

When we say yes to God's call of love, we are released from so many things; and our freedom in Christ is a wonderful gift to be enjoyed. But we too will likely be led to places we had not intended to go. Disciples of Jesus do have great freedom in Christ, and they also have great loyalty to the way of Christ. Consequently, they are often called to action and restraint as they stay in love with God and seek to live a life of faithfulness, fidelity, and integrity. (Job, *Three Simple Rules*, 55, 61)

Taking Time to Reflect

 Pause and recall what you have read and heard, as well as your own life experiences. Take note of anything that particularly catches your attention—perhaps a word, phrase, or image.

Making Our Requests Known

Focus your prayers more specifically on particular things, persons, or circumstances. The following petitions offer guidance:

Prayers for God's Creation and Our World
Prayers for All God's People
Prayers for the Church and All Who Seek God
Prayers for Our Neighbors
Prayers for Our Families and Friends
Prayers for Ourselves

Thanking God for Our Prayers and Life

Loving God,
I will accept and
cherish my relationship
as your beloved and
loving child
as I live a life of prayer
in your presence
today.

Prayer at the End of the Day

Inviting God's Activity

Tender Shepherd of my soul, make yourself and your way known to me in this evening time of prayer and reflection. By the power of your presence, bring me to the end of the day whole, complete, and at peace with you, my neighbor, and myself. Grant a night of peaceful rest and send me forth tomorrow as a witness to your love and grace.

A Continuing Request

Create a clean heart for me, God;
> put a new, faithful spirit deep inside me! (Psalm 51:10)

Gathering the Day

Remembering—Reflect on the day's experiences.

Confessing—Own up to your own weakness, failure, and sin.

Forgiving—Ask for and accept God's forgiveness, and forgive yourself and all who may have injured you or those you love.

Thanksgiving—Give thanks for the gifts that God has granted this day.

Offering

My whole being clings to you;
> your strong hand upholds me. (Psalm 63:8)

Blessing

I will lie down and fall asleep in peace
> because you alone, Lord, let me live in safety. (Psalm 4:8)

Week 26

A Faithful Walk

Approaching God with Intention

Loving God,
I offer open hands,
open mind, open heart,
and a willing spirit
to hear continually
your calling and sending voice.
I abandon my life into your care
with the assurance that you
will lead me in paths
of righteousness and goodness.
Amen.

 Sit in silence and stillness for a few moments, lengthening the time each day if you are able.

Becoming Aware of God's Presence

You are my God—I will give thanks to you!
    You are my God—I will lift you up high!
Give thanks to the LORD because he is good,
    because his faithful love lasts forever. (Psalm 118:28-29)

Inviting God's Intervention

LORD, let your faithful love come to me—
> let your salvation come to me according to your promise.
>> (Psalm 119:41)

Listening for God's Voice

Open yourself to hear what God is saying to you through the Scriptures.

"Whoever is faithful with little is also faithful with much, and the one who is dishonest with little is also dishonest with much. If you haven't been faithful with worldly wealth, who will trust you with true riches? If you haven't been faithful with someone else's property, who will give you your own? No household servant can serve two masters. Either you will hate the one and love the other, or you will be loyal to the one and have contempt for the other. You cannot serve God and wealth." (Luke 16:10-13)

Alternative Readings
John 15:1-8
Acts 11:19-26
Psalm 119:90-92
2 Timothy 4:1-8
Acts 8:26-40
John 17:6-19

Practicing Spiritual Reading

As you read the essay and one or more quotations each day, do so with an openness for further contemplation on the week's theme. Ask God, Is there a word or prayer for my life in these words?

More than twenty-five years ago a friend asked me how he should pray for me as my family and I were preparing to move to another state. I responded, "Pray that I may be faithful in all things." As soon as I finished signing a book for him, he wrote my prayer request next to my signature. Recently, we had a wonderful reunion and as we parted he said, "How should I pray for you now that you are retired?" My response was nearly automatic, "Pray that I may remain faithful." He pulled out the well-used Guide to Prayer that I had signed twenty-five years ago and opened it to where I had signed and he had written my prayer request. They were the same. My desire for faithfulness then was as intense as my desire for water on a hot summer day. A lot has changed since then. I have seen failure and success, loss and gain, and more times than I wish I have failed to live up to my own prayer and that of my friend. But I can tell you that long years with the same prayer always close to the surface of my mind and heart has led me on a very formative and fulfilling path. It is a path I plan to follow as long as I live. What are your plans?

 The end of all Christian belief and obedience, witness and teaching, marriage and family, leisure and work life, preaching and pastoral work is the living of everything we know about God: life, life, and more life. If we don't know where we are going, any road will get us there. But if we have a destination—in this case a life lived to the glory of God—there is a well-marked way, the Jesus-revealed Way. (Eugene H. Peterson, *Christ Plays in Ten Thousand Places: A Conversation in Spiritual Theology*, 1.)

The powers of this world do not want to see their authority and control usurped by another, even if that other is God. To preach a message and practice a life of authentic discipleship will make us uncomfortable and make others anxious and sometimes hostile. We are not above the struggle of what it means to follow Jesus. The complex issues of life do not lend themselves to easy answers. It is not easy to know with certainty the path we are to follow. And often, after careful discernment, the direction we hear is not the way we would have chosen. There is often resistance within us to the way we are convinced God is calling us to travel. It is a strenuous journey of faith that permits us to say with Mary, "Here I am, the servant of the Lord; let it be with me according to your word" (Luke 1:38 NRSV). (Job, *A Wesleyan Spiritual Reader*, 172.)

While pursuing the business of the day, we cannot ignore the Spirit inspired nudges we feel to examine its ups and downs in a prayerful way: . . . When distractions tap like raindrops against the windowpanes of our mind, we renew our attention and turn toward the Holy. In due time we may experience a deeper calm, a miracle of grace, words fail to convey. (Susan Muto, *Late Have I Loved Thee: The Recovery of Intimacy*, 119.)

Whatever is reported of Jesus . . . is to be replicated in us. Just go through the Gospels and find out what he is like. It's a revelation of what is in store for you, what is expected of you, what is promised to you, and what you in your profoundest reality always already are. (Beatrice Bruteau, *Radical Optimism: Rooting Ourselves in Reality*, 91.)

Taking Time to Reflect

Pause and recall what you have read and heard, as well as your own life experiences. Take note of anything that particularly catches your attention—perhaps a word, phrase, or image.

Making Our Requests Known

Focus your prayers more specifically on particular things, persons, or circumstances. The following petitions offer guidance:

Prayers for God's Creation and Our World
Prayers for All God's People
Prayers for the Church and All Who Seek God
Prayers for Our Neighbors
Prayers for Our Families and Friends
Prayers for Ourselves

Thanking God for Our Prayers and Life

Loving God,
Thank you
For hearing my prayers
And accepting my life.
I offer them to you
As completely as I can.
In the Name and Spirit of Jesus Christ.
Amen.

Prayer at the End of the Day

Inviting God's Activity

Tender Shepherd of my soul, make yourself and your way known to me in this evening time of prayer and reflection. By the power of your presence, bring me to the end of the day whole, complete, and at peace with you, my neighbor, and myself. Grant a night of peaceful rest and send me forth tomorrow as a witness to your love and grace.

A Continuing Request

Create a clean heart for me, God;
> put a new, faithful spirit deep inside me! (Psalm 51:10)

Gathering the Day

Remembering—Reflect on the day's experiences.

Confessing—Own up to your own weakness, failure, and sin.

Forgiving—Ask for and accept God's forgiveness, and forgive yourself and all who may have injured you or those you love.

Thanksgiving—Give thanks for the gifts that God has granted this day.

Offering

My whole being clings to you;
> your strong hand upholds me. (Psalm 63:8)

Blessing

I will lie down and fall asleep in peace
> because you alone, Lord, let me live in safety. (Psalm 4:8)

Week 27

Always in God's Presence

Approaching God with Intention

Holy God
>of unconditional love
>and unlimited presence,
>I come to make myself fully available
>to you, your will, and your way.

Speak to me gently and clearly,
>for I am yours
>and desire to hear, understand,
>and be obedient
>to your slightest whisper.

Speak, for I am listening.

 Sit in silence and stillness for a few moments, lengthening the time each day if you are able.

Becoming Aware of God's Presence

>The Companion, the Holy Spirit, whom the Father will send in my name, will teach you everything and will remind you of everything I told you. (John 14:26)

Inviting God's Intervention

Come Holy Spirit, and do your good and mighty work within and through this day!

Listening for God's Voice

Open yourself to hear what God is saying to you through the Scriptures.

> "If you love me, you will keep my commandments. I will ask the Father, and he will send another Companion, who will be with you forever. This Companion is the Spirit of Truth, whom the world can't receive because it neither sees him nor recognizes him. You know him, because he lives with you and will be with you.

> "I won't leave you as orphans. I will come to you. Soon the world will no longer see me, but you will see me. Because I live, you will live too. On that day you will know that I am in my Father, you are in me, and I am in you. Whoever has my commandments and keeps them loves me. Whoever loves me will be loved by my Father, and I will love them and reveal myself to them."
> (John 14:15-21)

Alternative Readings
Romans 8:12-17
Isaiah 40:1-10
1 John 2:1-6
1 John 2:7-11
Acts 1:1-5
Philippians 1:3-11

Practicing Spiritual Reading

As you read the essay and one or more quotations each day, do so with an openness for further contemplation on the week's theme. Ask God, Is there a word or prayer for my life in these words?

Our hearts race and we are nearly overcome with awe, wonder, and joy when we permit the words of Jesus to even get close to our center of awareness. "Those who love me will keep my word, and my Father will love them, and we will come to them and make our home with them" (John 14:23 NRSV). That God chooses to "live with us" is almost too much for us to comprehend. It takes getting used to. It requires a reordering of our ideas about God and about ourselves. Even as you read these words, God is there with you to engage, reveal, guide, comfort, and companion. To remember this truth is to have our lives transformed. To forget it is to risk the danger of falling into fear and anxiety about today and tomorrow. To remember this truth is to face each day, no matter how difficult, or joyful, aware that God's loving and life-giving presence is with us always, and nothing can ever separate us from that presence. Let's remind each other that God has chosen to live with us always as we help each other to live faithfully in the light of that eternal Presence.

 We can accuse Jesus of many things, but we cannot accuse him of neglecting his relationship with God. He must have learned early how important it was to stay close to God if he was to fulfill his mission in the world. He must have learned early that there was power available to live the faithful, the fruitful, the good life and that this power involved staying connected, staying in touch, and staying in love with his trusted Abba (Mark 14:36; Romans 8:15). He found not only his strength and guidance but his greatest joy in communion, companionship with his loving Abba. Perhaps it was these experiences that prompted his teaching about prayer and faithfulness. (Job, *Three Simple Rules*, 56.)

I need the darkness in order to grow closer to God. Perhaps I am like a night-blooming flower that requires darkness to open my blossoms. In the darkness, I am more fully open to the One who has created me. The darkness has many gifts to offer us if we are willing to enter it. There are painful and scary things in the darkness but there is also creation and rebirth. There is promise and enlightenment. There is transformation and revelation. Most of all, in the darkness we may encounter the God for whom darkness and light are both alike. (Tara Soughers, *Treasures of Darkness: Finding God When Hope Is Hidden*, quoted in Job, *When You Pray* 2009, 115.)

I spent the early years on a farm in North Dakota. I fell in love with the prairies and with windmills. Our farm was surrounded with huge cottonwood trees that often sheltered our windmill from light breezes that would have otherwise turned it to face the wind and permitted it to do its assigned work of pumping water for the farm. When the breeze was too light to turn the huge fan into the wind, my father would climb the tall tower and physically turn the fan and tail of the windmill until it faced directly into the wind. Properly positioned, the slightest breeze was translated into life-giving water. Personal [prayer] can be a time of repositioning ourselves, a time of intentionally turning toward God. (Job, *A Guide to Retreat*, 12.)

Taking Time to Reflect

 Pause and recall what you have read and heard, as well as your own life experiences. Take note of anything that particularly catches your attention—perhaps a word, phrase, or image.

Making Our Requests Known

Focus your prayers more specifically on particular things, persons, or circumstances. The following petitions offer guidance:

Prayers for God's Creation and Our World
Prayers for All God's People
Prayers for the Church and All Who Seek God
Prayers for Our Neighbors
Prayers for Our Families and Friends
Prayers for Ourselves

Thanking God for Our Prayers and Life

I will bless the LORD at all times;
　　his praise will always be in my mouth.
I praise the LORD—
　　let the suffering listen and rejoice.
Magnify the LORD with me!
　　Together let us lift his name up high!
I sought the LORD and he answered me.
　　He delivered me from all my fears.
Those who look to God will shine;
　　their faces are never ashamed. (Psalm 34:1-5)

Prayer at the End of the Day

Inviting God's Activity

Tender Shepherd of my soul, make yourself and your way known to me in this evening time of prayer and reflection. By the power of your presence, bring me to the end of the day whole, complete, and at peace with you, my neighbor, and myself. Grant a night of peaceful rest and send me forth tomorrow as a witness to your love and grace.

A Continuing Request

Create a clean heart for me, God;
> put a new, faithful spirit deep inside me! (Psalm 51:10)

Gathering the Day

Remembering—Reflect on the day's experiences.

Confessing—Own up to your own weakness, failure, and sin.

Forgiving—Ask for and accept God's forgiveness, and forgive yourself and all who may have injured you or those you love.

Thanksgiving—Give thanks for the gifts that God has granted this day.

Offering

My whole being clings to you;
> your strong hand upholds me. (Psalm 63:8)

Blessing

I will lie down and fall asleep in peace
> because you alone, LORD, let me live in safety. (Psalm 4:8)

Week 28

Jesus Prays for Our Unity

Approaching God with Intention

Loving Teacher,
Help us to open our minds, hearts,
and entire lives to you.
Come, speak to us,
Teach us,
Lead us,
and form us
until we are more and more like you,
For we are yours.

 Sit in silence and stillness for a few moments, lengthening the time each day if you are able.

Becoming Aware of God's Presence

> But I was still always with you!
> You held my strong hand!
> You have guided me with your advice;
> later you will receive me with glory.
> Do I have anyone else in heaven?
> There's nothing on earth I desire except you.
>   (Psalm 73:23-25)

Inviting God's Intervention

Shepherd of Israel, listen! . . .
Wake up your power!
    Come to save us!
Restore us, God!
    Make your face shine so that we can be saved!
                     (Psalm 80:1a, 2b-3)

Listening for God's Voice

Open yourself to hear what God is saying to you through the Scriptures.

Therefore, as a prisoner for the Lord, I encourage you to live as people worthy of the call you received from God. Conduct yourselves with all humility, gentleness, and patience. Accept each other with love, and make an effort to preserve the unity of the Spirit with the peace that ties you together. You are one body and one spirit, just as God also called you in one hope. There is one Lord, one faith, one baptism, and one God and Father of all, who is over all, through all, and in all.

Alternative Readings
Psalm 133
John 17:1-11
Ephesians 3:1-6
Psalm 68:1-10, 32-35
1 Peter 1:17-21
Revelation 22:12-14, 16-17, 20-21

God has given his grace to each one of us measured out by the gift that is given by Christ. That's why scripture says, *When he climbed up to the heights, he captured prisoners, and he gave gifts to people.* (Ephesians 4:1-8)

Practicing Spiritual Reading

As you read the essay and one or more quotations each day, do so with an openness for further contemplation on the week's theme. Ask God, Is there a word or prayer for my life in these words?

We live in a sharply divided world, and there are those who seem to feed on and delight in driving wedges of division wherever they can. We see it in communities, and we see it in congregations and denominations. One thing is obvious, and that is that those who seek to drive these wedges of division don't hang around Jesus much. Jesus was not afraid to speak the truth no matter where that truth touched his listeners. But his life was given to heal the wounds of division, and his prayer recorded in John 17 is an emphatic reminder of his determination to see divisions healed and unity restored: "Holy Father, protect them in your name that you have given me, so that they may be one, as we are one" (John 17:11b NRSV).

What would our world be like if this prayer of Jesus was answered today? What changes would we see in our communities and our congregations? We do not know all that would happen, but we do know that the changes would be dramatic, life-giving, and liberating. Let us pray that the prayer of Jesus will be answered in our time and where we live. And then let us promise God and one another every day that each of us will become a living answer to this fervent prayer of Jesus. It will change our world!

 We rise from prayer transformed because we have been intimately involved with the One who not only gives us life but also transforms our lives while leading us further and further into that grand design that God has for each of us. (Job, *Three Simple Questions*, 46.)

What we have most in common is not religion but humanity. I learned this from my religion, which also teaches me that encountering another human being is as close to God as I may ever get—in the eye-to-eye thing, the person-to-person thing—which is where God's Beloved has promised to show up. Paradoxically, the point is not to see him. The point is to see the person standing right in front of me, who has no substitute, who can never be replaced, whose heart holds things for which there is no language, whose life is an unsolved mystery. (Taylor, *An Altar in the World*, 102.)

Honesty requires us to invite God's Spirit to examine us and see where, how, and when we contribute to our brokenness as the body of Christ. What is it in us that makes it so difficult to see others as children of God who are loved by God and accepted by God as we believe we are loved and accepted by God? This was an issue for the Twelve and for the early followers of Jesus, just as it is an issue for us. . . .

But as the church listened to the Holy Spirit, they learned that the circle of the community that was being invited to follow Jesus was larger and more inclusive than anyone had imagined, and they were able to change and become an open and inviting community. (Job, *Three Simple Questions*, 58–59.)

The divine ratification we need is that which comes with the good news that God really does love all people without exception, that God loves "us," and, most importantly, that God loves me! The heartwarming part of the Good News is that we do not have to come to this stunning truth all by ourselves. As we make our efforts to reach out and be open to this loving God, God is already there helping us. This is grace: "I am here; I am with you; I love you; I will never let you go!" (Richard M. Gula, S. S., *To Walk Together Again: The Sacrament of Reconciliation*, 58.)

Taking Time to Reflect

Pause and recall what you have read and heard, as well as your own life experiences. Take note of anything that particularly catches your attention—perhaps a word, phrase, or image.

Making Our Requests Known

Focus your prayers more specifically on particular things, persons, or circumstances. The following petitions offer guidance:

Prayers for God's Creation and Our World
Prayers for All God's People
Prayers for the Church and All Who Seek God
Prayers for Our Neighbors
Prayers for Our Families and Friends
Prayers for Ourselves

Thanking God for Our Prayers and Life

Tender Shepherd,
Gather us together as your flock,
Lead us in paths of righteousness,
    justice, peace, unity, and love,
And grant us grace to follow faithfully.
In the Name and Spirit of Jesus Christ.
Amen.

Prayer at the End of the Day

Inviting God's Activity

Tender Shepherd of my soul, make yourself and your way known to me in this evening time of prayer and reflection. By the power of your presence, bring me to the end of the day whole, complete, and at peace with you, my neighbor, and myself. Grant a night of peaceful rest and send me forth tomorrow as a witness to your love and grace.

A Continuing Request

Create a clean heart for me, God;
    put a new, faithful spirit deep inside me! (Psalm 51:10)

Gathering the Day

Remembering—Reflect on the day's experiences.

Confessing—Own up to your own weakness, failure, and sin.

Forgiving—Ask for and accept God's forgiveness, and forgive yourself and all who may have injured you or those you love.

Thanksgiving—Give thanks for the gifts that God has granted this day.

Offering

My whole being clings to you;
    your strong hand upholds me. (Psalm 63:8)

Blessing

I will lie down and fall asleep in peace
    because you alone, Lord, let me live in safety. (Psalm 4:8)

Week 29

Power Beyond Our Own

Approaching God with Intention

Creator God,
deepen our awareness of your
mighty acts past and present
and your constant presence
with us every moment
of our existence
because we want to know you
and remember who you are
with every breath we take. Amen.

 Sit in silence and stillness for a few moments, lengthening the time each day if you are able.

Becoming Aware of God's Presence

> When God began to create the heavens and the earth—the earth was without shape or form, it was dark over the deep sea, and God's wind swept over the waters. (Genesis 1:1-2)

Inviting God's Intervention

> Make them holy in the truth; your word is truth. As you sent me into the world, so I have sent them into the world.
>
> (John 17:17-18)

Listening for God's Voice

Open yourself to hear what God is saying to you through the Scriptures.

You will eat abundantly and be satisfied,
>> and you will praise the name of the LORD your God,
> who has done wonders for you;
>> and my people will never again be put to shame.

You will know that I am in the midst of Israel,
>> and that I am the LORD your God—no other exists;
>> never again will my people be put to shame.

After that I will pour out my spirit upon everyone;
>> your sons and your daughters will prophesy,
>> your old men will dream dreams,
>> and your young men will see visions.

In those days, I will also pour out my
> spirit on the male and female slaves.

(Joel 2:26-29)

Alternative Readings

1 John 4:1-6

John 20:19-23

Psalm 104:24-34

Acts 20:17-24

2 Corinthians 1:12-22

Romans 8:22-27

Practicing Spiritual Reading

As you read the essay and one or more quotations each day, do so with an openness for further contemplation on the week's theme. Ask God, Is there a word or prayer for my life in these words?

While serving as a district superintendent, I often asked congregations what they were planning for the next year that could not be accomplished without God's intervention. The Bible is filled with stories of accomplishments that were achieved only as God's people sought, accepted, and invested power from beyond themselves, God's power to achieve their God-honored goals. Far too often we try to do far too much on our own, forgetting that there is help available from the One who made us, loves us, and walks with us in all of life's experiences. Today, instead of getting stressed out because I have too much to do, I will ask God to guide me in my yes and no to tasks and opportunities that come my way. And then I will ask God to inspire, bless, and grant wisdom, energy, and strength beyond my own to do what God has placed in my hands to accomplish. How will you approach the opportunities and tasks that await you?

The good news we share with each other as followers of Jesus Christ is that God's love and grace sweep across us all the time. We may not be aware of it because we are preoccupied, there is too much that is distracting us or we are just not paying attention. But it is impossible for us to avoid, hide from, escape, or be left out of God's grace that is sweeping across us all the time. (Job, *Life Stories*, 66.)

I believe that prayer is all about our relationship with a God who loves us. Prayer is the way we connect and stay connected to God. We enter into this relationship at the urging of God. God wants an ongoing, vibrant, loving relationship with all of us. God desires us not because we are good or holy or set apart in any way; God calls all of us, just as we are, into relationship and offers us the possibility of intimacy. (Vennard, *A Praying Congregation*, 42.)

Far too often we are content with a god who offers a band-aid for our wounded souls rather than the God of radical mercy, justice, and love—who forgives our sins and wipes them away just as soon as we offer that same forgiveness to those who may have wronged us; who not only forgives our sins but also heals our wounded souls, mends our broken relationships, and sends us on our way full of hope, confidence, trust, and strength to transform the world by living in the kingdom of God already being formed "on earth as it is in heaven." (Job, *Three Simple Questions*, 17.)

After we have been awakened to the presence of the Spirit, a new moment arises in our spiritual life. Our effort is now directed to responding to the internal law of the Spirit written in our heart rather than simply conforming to the external obligations as they have been presented to us by the authorities in our life. We do indeed continue to fulfill these obligations, but our reasons have been more deeply internalized. And responding to the Spirit is a far more challenging project. It demands that we habitually live in tune with our inner experiences, distinguishing those which flow from the Spirit from those that do not. (Richard J. Hauser, *Moving in the Spirit: Becoming a Contemplative in Action*, 23.)

Taking Time to Reflect

 Pause and recall what you have read and heard, as well as your own life experiences. Take note of anything that particularly catches your attention—perhaps a word, phrase, or image.

Making Our Requests Known

Focus your prayers more specifically on particular things, persons, or circumstances. The following petitions offer guidance:

Prayers for God's Creation and Our World
Prayers for All God's People
Prayers for the Church and All Who Seek God
Prayers for Our Neighbors
Prayers for Our Families and Friends
Prayers for Ourselves

Thanking God for Our Prayers and Life

God of love
beyond my comprehension,
hold me close so that I may be
as aware of the beat of your heart of love
as I am of the beat of my own heart
as you guide me through the day.

Prayer at the End of the Day

Inviting God's Activity

Tender Shepherd of my soul, make yourself and your way known to me in this evening time of prayer and reflection. By the power of your presence, bring me to the end of the day whole, complete, and at peace with you, my neighbor, and myself. Grant a night of peaceful rest and send me forth tomorrow as a witness to your love and grace.

A Continuing Request

Create a clean heart for me, God;
    put a new, faithful spirit deep inside me! (Psalm 51:10)

Gathering the Day

Remembering—Reflect on the day's experiences.

Confessing—Own up to your own weakness, failure, and sin.

Forgiving—Ask for and accept God's forgiveness, and forgive yourself and all who may have injured you or those you love.

Thanksgiving—Give thanks for the gifts that God has granted this day.

Offering

My whole being clings to you;
    your strong hand upholds me. (Psalm 63:8)

Blessing

I will lie down and fall asleep in peace
    because you alone, LORD, let me live in safety. (Psalm 4:8)

Week 30

God Made Known

Approaching God with Intention

Creator of all that exists
and lover of all you have made,
Bless me with eyes to see your presence
in the world you love,
Ears to hear your tender voice
of guidance,
And courage to say,
"Here I am, use me this day
for I am yours."

 Sit in silence and stillness for a few moments, lengthening the time each day if you are able.

Becoming Aware of God's Presence

Rejoice and be glad, Daughter Zion,
  because I am about to come and dwell among you, says the
  Lord.
Many nations will be joined to the Lord on that day.
  They will become my people,
    and I will dwell among you
    so you will know that the Lord of heavenly forces sent me
to you." (Zechariah 2:10-11)

Inviting God's Intervention

> But you, LORD! Don't be far away!
>> You are my strength!
>> Come quick and help me! (Psalm 22:19)

Listening for God's Voice

Open yourself to hear what God is saying to you through the Scriptures.

> I will thank you, LORD, with all my heart;
>> I will talk about all your wonderful acts.
> I will celebrate and rejoice in you;
>> I will sing praises to your name, Most High.
> When my enemies turn and retreat,
>> they fall down and die right in front of you
>> because you have established justice
>>> for me and my claim,
>> because you rule from the throne,
>>> establishing justice rightly.
> You've denounced the nations,
>> destroyed the wicked.
>> You've erased their names for all time. . . .
> The LORD is a safe place for the oppressed—
>> a safe place in difficult times. (Psalm 9:1-5, 9)

Alternative Readings

Philippians 2:1-11
Luke 24:44-49
Isaiah 44:1-8
Matthew 28:16-20
Micah 4:1-5
John 6:41-51

Practicing Spiritual Reading

As you read the essay and one or more quotations each day, do so with an openness for further contemplation on the week's theme. Ask God, Is there a word or prayer for my life in these words?

Beverly and I met in a college English class taught by a favorite professor. We had known each other for three years when we married and thought we really knew all about each other. Now, fifty-six years later, we are still making discoveries about who we are as individuals and about who we are together.

God's introduction (self-disclosure) began when humankind was first created. That self-disclosure has continued, and while God is still Mystery, we have come to know God as One, revealed as Father, Son, and Holy Spirit. Much of the Christian community celebrates Trinity Sunday as we continue to try to get to know more fully the One who created all that is, gives us life, redeems us, and chooses to walk with us always to comfort, guide, sustain, defend, and lead us safely to our eternal home. Until that final "Welcome Home," I intend to continue getting acquainted, getting to know, and building a life-giving relationship with the God who has chosen to let us experience Divine Presence every day. What are your intentions?

There was a time when most people could see a starry sky, a beautiful sunrise, and the bursting creativity of God in all of nature. But with massive population growth, migration to the cities of the world, and artificial light that blinds us to the wonder and mystery of creation, we look for other places to see God's handiwork unfold.

Today as you see the face of another, a bit of the sky, or a flourishing plant, remember the Creator God who upholds all that is and give thanks for daily evidence of that presence in our distracted world. (Job, *Three Simple Questions*, 31.)

> Holy Trinity,
> Mystery of loving communion,
> Invitation to deeper union.
> Grant me the grace to pass
> The test of trust.
> Teach me to be self-donating,
> To express freely
> A commitment to mutuality,
> To ever loving,
> Quietly befriending reciprocity.
> Strengthen my will to love
> My sisters and brothers
> As you love us and all others. (Muto, *Late Have I Loved Thee*, 23.)

Now Jesus himself was and is a joyous, creative person. He does not allow us to continue thinking of our Father who fills and overflows space as a morose and miserable monarch, a frustrated and petty parent, or a policeman on prowl. One cannot think of God in such ways while confronting Jesus' declaration, "He that has seen me has seen the Father." (Willard, *The Divine Conspiracy*, 64.)

"Holiness," said Walter Rauschenbusch, "is goodness on fire." This captures well the holiness—and the danger—of Jesus, his power to attract and disturb . . . before re-creation or redemption can occur. . . . Most of us, along with our culture, create some tamer, more easily contained version of Jesus and the holiness he represents. A Jesus who becomes easy to laugh at, shrug off, dismiss. . . . Not a person, not the living God who speaks and rattles the foundations of the earth. (Joy Jordan-Lake, *Why Jesus Makes Me Nervous: Ten Alarming Words of Faith*, 44.)

Taking Time to Reflect

 Pause and recall what you have read and heard, as well as your own life experiences. Take note of anything that particularly catches your attention—perhaps a word, phrase, or image.

Making Our Requests Known

Focus your prayers more specifically on particular things, persons, or circumstances. The following petitions offer guidance:

Prayers for God's Creation and Our World
Prayers for All God's People
Prayers for the Church and All Who Seek God
Prayers for Our Neighbors
Prayers for Our Families and Friends
Prayers for Ourselves

Thanking God for Our Prayers and Life

It is good to give thanks to the LORD,
      to sing praises to your name, Most High;
      to proclaim your loyal love in the morning,
         your faithfulness at nighttime . . .
      because you've made me happy, LORD,
      by your acts. (Psalm 92:1-2, 4a)

Prayer at the End of the Day

Inviting God's Activity

Tender Shepherd of my soul, make yourself and your way known to me in this evening time of prayer and reflection. By the power of your presence, bring me to the end of the day whole, complete, and at peace with you, my neighbor, and myself. Grant a night of peaceful rest and send me forth tomorrow as a witness to your love and grace.

A Continuing Request

Create a clean heart for me, God;
     put a new, faithful spirit deep inside me! (Psalm 51:10)

Gathering the Day

Remembering—Reflect on the day's experiences.

Confessing—Own up to your own weakness, failure, and sin.

Forgiving—Ask for and accept God's forgiveness, and forgive yourself and all who may have injured you or those you love.

Thanksgiving—Give thanks for the gifts that God has granted this day.

Offering

My whole being clings to you;
     your strong hand upholds me. (Psalm 63:8)

Blessing

I will lie down and fall asleep in peace
     because you alone, LORD, let me live in safety. (Psalm 4:8)

Prayer Practice

Lectio Divina—Meditation on Scripture

For centuries meditation has been associated with holy reading, or lectio divina. Lectio divina is the practice of reading a section of Scripture and then meditating and praying on it. This ancient prayer practice helps us to listen for and understand God's revelation as it restores and renews our trust in and love for God.

Each day you are encouraged to select a portion of a daily Scripture passage and meditate on it for at least five minutes (ten to fifteen minutes would be ideal).

Read the passage slowly and make notes of anything that seems significant. Think deeply about the text, visualizing any scenes or writing about your understanding of the passage. Pray about what it means for you specifically. Sit silently, listening and communing with God.

Meditating on God's revelation in creation can also be a restorative practice. Take a walk or sit outside and observe the beauty of God's creation. Both of these ways of meditating on God's revelation can open us to the Holy Spirit's desire to invade our mind and heart and further develop our relationship with God as revealed in Jesus Christ. Take time each day to meditate on God's revelation, allowing your soul to be renewed and refreshed. (Job, *Listen*, 70.)

Week 31

Go Where the Wounds Are

Approaching God with Intention

Lover of all who are lost,
Uncertain and alone,
Anxious and fearful,
All who are seeking a safe and secure home,
Come to me now
So that I may recognize and welcome your voice
Embrace your presence,
And invite you to change me more and more
Into that wonderful image you have of me
As your faithful, loving, and obedient child. Amen.

 Sit in silence and stillness for a few moments, lengthening the time each day if you are able.

Becoming Aware of God's Presence

Living in the Most High's shelter,
   camping in the Almighty's shade,
I say to the LORD, "You are my refuge, my stronghold!
   You are my God—the one I trust!" (Psalm 91:1-2)

Inviting God's Intervention

Remember me, LORD, with the favor you show your people.
> Visit me with your saving help
>> so I can experience the good things your chosen ones
>> experience,
>> so I can rejoice in the joy of your nation,
>> so I can praise along with your possession. (Psalm 106:4-5)

Listening for God's Voice

Open yourself to hear what God is saying to you through the Scriptures.

While Jesus was speaking to them, a ruler came and knelt in front of him, saying, "My daughter has just died. But come and place your hand on her, and she'll live." So Jesus and his disciples got up and went with him. Then a woman who had been bleeding for twelve years came up behind Jesus and touched the hem of his clothes. She thought, If I only touch his robe I'll be healed.

When Jesus turned and saw her, he said, "Be encouraged, daughter. Your faith has healed you." And the woman was healed from that time on.

When Jesus went into the ruler's house, he saw the flute players and the distressed crowd. He said, "Go away, because the little girl isn't dead but is asleep"; but they laughed at him. After he had sent the crowd away, Jesus went in and touched her hand, and the little girl rose up. News about this spread throughout that whole region.

(Matthew 9:18-26)

Alternative Readings

Matthew 11:2-6
Acts 5:12-16
Mark 2:23–3:6
Acts 3:1-10
Luke 7:1-10
Acts 14: 8-18

Practicing Spiritual Reading

As you read the essay and one or more quotations each day, do so with an openness for further contemplation on the week's theme. Ask God, Is there a word or prayer for my life in these words?

Want to follow Jesus? Go where the wounds are, for that is where Jesus went. Demon-possessed, paralyzed, blind, cut off from family and community, ostracized and left out, ridiculed and harassed, divided and estranged, these were the ones who seemed to draw the very presence of Jesus. And not only draw his presence but experience his healing, peace-producing, and life-giving power. Jesus had the ability to show up where the wounds seemed to be greatest, and those who heard of him seemed to show up wherever he was to receive the gift of healing.

We don't have to be particularly observant to notice that our world is filled with the wounded and broken. While many of them may feel forgotten, estranged, ridiculed, and left out, they are the very ones to whom Jesus comes to bring healing, hope, and wholeness.

Would you like to experience a new level of effectiveness and faithfulness? Go where the wounds are. This is what Jesus did and that is what Jesus does today. Let's meet him there today and every day and be a part of his life-giving ministry.

Compassion and a concern for social justice come from the nature of God as seen clearly in Exodus. This is indeed a challenge, for not only are we to hear the cry of those who are suffering in our day but we are also to act for their liberation whenever this is possible. Jesus' instruction, "Be compassionate, as your Father is compassionate" (Luke 6:36, NAB), takes us directly to prayer, for without God's help we could never approach this depth of compassion and care. (Oliva, *Free to Pray, Free to Love*, 105–106.)

The life of Jesus Christ witnessed to God's infinite caring for the very hairs of our heads, and for the lost sheep. It is no accident, therefore, that in prayer, in the presence of Jesus Christ, we are brought inwardly before the revolutionary levelling of God's infinite concern for every soul that comes into the world. "Christianity taught us to care. Caring is the greatest thing—caring matters most." These words of [Baron Friedrich] von Hügel's are borne out in Christian prayer; for to come into the field of force of God's infinite caring is to feel inwardly the terrible pull of the unlimited liability for one another that the New Testament ethic lays upon us. This lays the knife at the root of every claim for special privilege and of all "comfortism," and no amount of theological casuistry can justify our disregarding it. (Steere, *Dimensions of Prayer*, 106.)

Each of us knows of groups that are locked in conflict, sometimes over profound issues and sometimes over issues that are just plain silly. But the conflict is real, the divisions deep, and the consequences can often be devastating. If, however, all who are involved can agree to do no harm, the *climate* in which the conflict is going on is immediately changed. How is it changed? Well, if I am to do no harm, I can no longer *gossip* about the conflict. I can no longer *speak disparagingly* about those involved in the conflict. I can no longer *manipulate the facts* of the conflict. I can no longer *diminish* those who do not agree with me and must honor each as a child of God. (Job, *Three Simple Rules*, 22.)

Taking Time to Reflect

 Pause and recall what you have read and heard, as well as your own life experiences. Take note of anything that particularly catches your attention—perhaps a word, phrase, or image.

Making Our Requests Known

Focus your prayers more specifically on particular things, persons, or circumstances. The following petitions offer guidance:

Prayers for God's Creation and Our World
Prayers for All God's People
Prayers for the Church and All Who Seek God
Prayers for Our Neighbors
Prayers for Our Families and Friends
Prayers for Ourselves

Thanking God for Our Prayers and Life

God,
Greater than anything I can imagine,
Holiness purer and more brilliant than light,
Mercy that forgives, redeems, and leads to righteousness,
Love that accepts and embraces me just as I am,
Grace that sustains and molds me into more than I am,
Promised presence that will never forsake me or leave me alone,
I declare that I am yours alone
And invite you to do with me what you will
As I walk in the light and life
Of your unfailing presence.

Prayer at the End of the Day

Inviting God's Activity

Tender Shepherd of my soul, make yourself and your way known to me in this evening time of prayer and reflection. By the power of your presence, bring me to the end of the day whole, complete, and at peace with you, my neighbor, and myself. Grant a night of peaceful rest and send me forth tomorrow as a witness to your love and grace.

A Continuing Request

Create a clean heart for me, God;
> put a new, faithful spirit deep inside me! (Psalm 51:10)

Gathering the Day

Remembering—Reflect on the day's experiences.

Confessing—Own up to your own weakness, failure, and sin.

Forgiving—Ask for and accept God's forgiveness, and forgive yourself and all who may have injured you or those you love.

Thanksgiving—Give thanks for the gifts that God has granted this day.

Offering

My whole being clings to you;
> your strong hand upholds me. (Psalm 63:8)

Blessing

I will lie down and fall asleep in peace
> because you alone, LORD, let me live in safety. (Psalm 4:8)

Week 32

Who Will Lead Us?

Approaching God with Intention

Teach me your way, LORD,
      so that I can walk in your truth.
     Make my heart focused
        only on honoring your name.
I give thanks to you, my Lord, my God,
with all my heart,
and I will glorify your name forever,
      because your faithful love toward me is awesome
     and because you've rescued my life
        from the lowest part of hell. (Psalm 86:11-13)

 Sit in silence and stillness for a few moments, lengthening the time each day if you are able.

Becoming Aware of God's Presence

LORD, you have examined me.
     You know me.
You know when I sit down and when I stand up.
     Even from far away, you comprehend my plans.
You study my traveling and resting.
     You are thoroughly familiar with all my ways.

                              (Psalm 139:1-3)

Inviting God's Intervention

Listen to my prayer, LORD!
> Because of your faithfulness, hear my requests for mercy!
> Because of your righteousness, answer me! (Psalm 143:1)

Listening for God's Voice

Open yourself to hear what God is saying to you through the Scriptures.

Now the boy Samuel was serving the LORD under Eli. The LORD's word was rare at that time, and visions weren't widely known. One day Eli, whose eyes had grown so weak he was unable to see, was lying down in his room. God's lamp hadn't gone out yet, and Samuel was lying down in the LORD's temple, where God's chest was.

The LORD called to Samuel. "I'm here," he said.

Samuel hurried to Eli and said, "I'm here. You called me?"

"I didn't call you," Eli replied. "Go lie down." So he did.

Again the LORD called Samuel, so Samuel got up, went to Eli, and said, "I'm here. You called me?"

"I didn't call, my son," Eli replied. "Go and lie down."

(Now Samuel didn't yet know the LORD, and the LORD's word hadn't yet been revealed to him.)

A third time the LORD called Samuel. He got up, went to Eli, and said, "I'm here. You called me?"

Then Eli realized that it was the LORD who was calling the boy. So Eli said to Samuel, "Go and lie down. If he calls you, say, 'Speak,

Alternative Readings
Luke 5:1-11
Hebrews 3:1-6
Genesis 6:1-22
Mark 1:16-20
Matthew 4:18-22
Acts 1:21-26

L̲ord̲. Your servant is listening.'" So Samuel went and lay down where he'd been.

Then the L̲ord̲ came and stood there, calling just as before, "Samuel, Samuel!"

Samuel said, "Speak. Your servant is listening." (1 Samuel 3:1-10)

Practicing Spiritual Reading

As you read the essay and one or more quotations each day, do so with an openness for further contemplation on the week's theme. Ask God, Is there a word or prayer for my life in these words?

When Jesus chose leaders he went way beyond the normal expectations that observers had assumed would shape the leaders of this new community. Here was the perfect opportunity to shape this new community that would become the church, and Jesus clearly seized the opportunity. His early choice of Matthew shocked the observers. I imagine no one expected Jesus to choose a wealthy tax collector and no one expected that such a person would give up everything and follow Jesus. And the shock waves grew greater when he went to dinner at this tax collector's home. Clearly, Jesus had the capacity to bridge the many, many chasms that were created to keep people apart, ignorant, and suspicious of each other.

I wonder how many times I have missed opportunities to choose leaders as Jesus did. Sometimes I may have been afraid to ask, thinking they would never agree to the radical requirements of the task. And at other times I was afraid to ask because I missed the enormous potential for leadership in persons who could by their very choice bridge chasms that keep people apart and therefore build strong communities of faith and mission. I would like to do better than I did in choosing faithful and effective leaders. How about you?

Ministry is not without cost. Christian ministry is to follow the selfless way of Christ. To say that we are followers of Christ, representatives of Christ, servants of Christ, and to expect ease, comfort, and our own way is indeed an unthinkable contradiction.

To follow One who wept and bled, who prayed and struggled, who went to parties and weddings, who associated with saints and sinners, who was loved and embraced, who was misunderstood and doubted, who was revered and rejected, who was followed and betrayed, and who, in the eyes of the world, utterly failed, is to place oneself in the pathway of similar experiences. The disciple is not above the teacher. (Job, *A Guide to Retreat*, 148.)

Integrated leaders *will* help people grow—just by being who they are. . . . Saying clearly who they are and where they stand, those leaders will encourage others to do the same, bringing all their experiences and the symbols of the tradition into enlivening conversation. . . . In this they follow One who called himself the Way (rather than the destination), and made conversations on the road the centerpiece of his leadership training. (Celia Allison Hahn, *Growing in Authority, Relinquishing Control: A New Approach to Faithful Leadership*, 174.)

For a Christian, Jesus is the man in whom it has indeed become manifest that revolution and conversion cannot be separated in man's search for experiential transcendence. His appearance in our midst has made it undeniably clear that changing the human heart and changing human society are not separate tasks, but are as interconnected as the two beams of the cross. Jesus was a revolutionary, who did not become an extremist, since he did not offer an ideology, but Himself. He was also a mystic, who did not use his intimate relationship with God to avoid the social evils of his time, but shocked his milieu to the point of being executed as a rebel. In this sense he also remains for nuclear man the way to liberation and freedom. (Henri J. M. Nouwen, *The Wounded Healer: Ministry in Contemporary Society*, 20–21.)

Taking Time to Reflect

Pause and recall what you have read and heard, as well as your own life experiences. Take note of anything that particularly catches your attention—perhaps a word, phrase, or image.

Making Our Requests Known

Focus your prayers more specifically on particular things, persons, or circumstances. The following petitions offer guidance:

Prayers for God's Creation and Our World
Prayers for All God's People
Prayers for the Church and All Who Seek God
Prayers for Our Neighbors
Prayers for Our Families and Friends
Prayers for Ourselves

Thanking God for Our Prayers and Life

Giver of every good and perfect gift,
once more I desire to offer myself
and my life to you.
Accept the offering I make
and lead me in paths of righteousness, goodness, and truth.
Amen.

Prayer at the End of the Day

Inviting God's Activity

Tender Shepherd of my soul, make yourself and your way known to me in this evening time of prayer and reflection. By the power of your presence, bring me to the end of the day whole, complete, and at peace with you, my neighbor and myself. Grant a night of peaceful rest and send me forth tomorrow as a witness to your love and grace.

A Continuing Request

Create a clean heart for me, God;
> put a new, faithful spirit deep inside me! (Psalm 51:10)

Gathering the Day

Remembering—Reflect on the day's experiences.

Confessing—Own up to your own weakness, failure, and sin.

Forgiving—Ask for and accept God's forgiveness, and forgive yourself and all who may have injured you or those you love.

Thanksgiving —Give thanks for the gifts that God has granted this day.

Offering

My whole being clings to you;
> your strong hand upholds me. (Psalm 63:8)

Blessing

I will lie down and fall asleep in peace
> because you alone, LORD, let me live in safety. (Psalm 4:8)

Week 33

What Will People Say?

Approaching God with Intention

Loving God,
Who understands before I form my prayer,
Who hears when I call and translates my humble words
into beautiful hymns of gratitude and praise,
Here I am as fully in your presence
as I am able to be
Offering my fears, my needs, my hopes,
my love, and my life. Amen.

 Sit in silence and stillness for a few moments, lengthening the time each day if you are able.

Becoming Aware of God's Presence

> Shine your face on your servant,
>> and teach me your statutes. (Psalm 119:135)

Inviting God's Intervention

> I've wandered off like a sheep, lost.
>> Find your servant
>>> because I haven't forgotten
>>> your commandments! (Psalm 119:176)

Listening for God's Voice

Open yourself to hear what God is saying to you through the Scriptures.

> What did you go out to see? A prophet? Yes, I tell you, and more than a prophet. He is the one of whom it's written: Look, I'm sending my messenger before you, who will prepare your way before you. I tell you that no greater human being has ever been born than John. Yet whoever is least in God's kingdom is greater than he." Everyone who heard this, including the tax collectors, acknowledged God's justice because they had been baptized by John. But the Pharisees and legal experts rejected God's will for themselves because they hadn't been baptized by John.

> "To what will I compare the people of this generation?" Jesus asked. "What are they like? They are like children sitting in the marketplace calling out to each other, 'We played the flute for you and you didn't dance. We sang a funeral song and you didn't cry.' John the Baptist came neither eating bread nor drinking wine, and you say, 'He has a demon.' Yet the Human One came eating and drinking, and you say, 'Look, a glutton and a drunk, a friend of tax collectors and sinners.' But wisdom is proved to be right by all her descendants." (Luke 7:26-35)

Alternative Readings

Luke 7:36–8:3

Matthew 11:7-19

Psalm 12

Galatians 2:11-14

Acts 11:1-18

Psalm 22:1-2, 7-11

Practicing Spiritual Reading

As you read the essay and one or more quotations each day, do so with an openness for further contemplation on the week's theme. Ask God, Is there a word or prayer for my life in these words?

Jesus got in trouble just by accepting an invitation to share a meal at the home of a Pharisee. But the real trouble began when a woman, identified by the people as a sinner, came and poured ointment on the feet of Jesus and wiped her tears from his feet with her hair (Luke 7:36-50). It was a remarkable and beautiful act of respect, reverence, gratitude, and affection. But the other guests didn't see it that way. Jesus wasn't swayed by the negative response of the other guests; rather he forgave and blessed the woman as he sent her on her way, forgiven and wrapped in the forgiveness of God.

My first appointment out of seminary was to a small congregation in a small town in central North Dakota. This little village had two grocery stores, two hardware stores, two filling stations, two churches, and two bars. One rainy afternoon, I decided to enter one of the bars to speak to one of the members of the congregation whose truck was parked out front. He was not the only member of the congregation present in the bar on that rainy afternoon, and, after greeting the rest and completing our brief conversation about a matter at the church, I made my way to other pastoral calls. By the next day, a common topic of conversation was my visit to the bar and being there with "those kind of people." I tried to shrug off the criticism, but it was difficult not to be intimidated by what people were saying. My prayer is that we may cultivate the capacity that Jesus demonstrated so clearly and embrace everyone as a child of God, worthy of all the gifts of God, including forgiveness and the opportunity of new beginnings.

 We want to know the truth! But truth is sometimes larger than words, even words skillfully put together. At other times truth is such strong medicine that we cannot take it unless it is carried in some other medium. Just as strong medicine is often carried within something else, so truth is sometimes best carried in story. A biblical example of this practice is found in 2 Samuel 12 as Nathan confronts David with his murderous act in order to gain another man's wife. Truth in story is not only made palatable as strong medicine in some carrier, but truth is often made understandable in story. Surely, this must be one reason Jesus used parables so often and so effectively to teach both ancient and new truths to those who followed him. (Job, *Life Stories*, 7.)

The law of the universe is that love never dies. It is written deep in the heart of creation and has been translated in many ways in a multitude of times and places. It is voiced by the prophets, telling us to write this law on the hearts of our children. It is preached by the apostles, saying that faith, hope, and love remain when everything else passes. It runs so deeply that people in exile for generations can still dream of love. In all religions, in all times, in all places, love holds humanity in a common good to God. It calls us to love God with all our hearts and minds and bodies, and to love our brothers and sisters as ourselves. (Becca Stevens, *Hither & Yon: A Travel Guide for the Spiritual Journey*, 135.)

We don't spend much time talking about sin in our culture. We should, however, for sin is real, contagious, and deadly. Unforgiven sin is a burden too heavy for any of us to carry. It leaves little room for joy and assurance in the life of a Christian. Unforgiven sin often lingers in the shadows of our lives, constantly reminding us of our inadequacy, our incompleteness, and our unworthiness. The longer we put off dealing with sin and forgiveness the more difficult it is to receive this free gift of grace. (Job, *A Wesleyan Spiritual Reader*, 116.)

Taking Time to Reflect

Pause and recall what you have read and heard, as well as your own life experiences. Take note of anything that particularly catches your attention—perhaps a word, phrase, or image.

Making Our Requests Known

Focus your prayers more specifically on particular things, persons, or circumstances. The following petitions offer guidance:

Prayers for God's Creation and Our World
Prayers for All God's People
Prayers for the Church and All Who Seek God
Prayers for Our Neighbors
Prayers for Our Families and Friends
Prayers for Ourselves

Thanking God for Our Prayers and Life

Loving God,
Remind me often today where I find my identity.
May I never forget that I am your beloved child.
Thank you for hearing my prayers
And accepting my life.
I offer them to you as completely as I can
In the Name and Spirit of Jesus Christ. Amen.

Prayer at the End of the Day

Inviting God's Activity

Tender Shepherd of my soul, make yourself and your way known to me in this evening time of prayer and reflection. By the power of your presence, bring me to the end of the day whole, complete, and at peace with you, my neighbor, and myself. Grant a night of peaceful rest and send me forth tomorrow as a witness to your love and grace.

A Continuing Request

Create a clean heart for me, God;
    put a new, faithful spirit deep inside me! (Psalm 51:10)

Gathering the Day

Remembering—Reflect on the day's experiences.

Confessing—Own up to your own weakness, failure, and sin.

Forgiving—Ask for and accept God's forgiveness, and forgive yourself and all who may have injured you or those you love.

Thanksgiving—Give thanks for the gifts that God has granted this day.

Offering

My whole being clings to you;
    your strong hand upholds me. (Psalm 63:8)

Blessing

I will lie down and fall asleep in peace
    because you alone, LORD, let me live in safety. (Psalm 4:8)

Week 34

Do Not Be Afraid

Approaching God with Intention

Save me, God,
because the waters have reached my neck!
I have sunk into deep mud.
My feet can't touch the bottom!
I have entered deep water;
the flood has swept me up.
I am tired of crying.
My throat is hoarse.
My eyes are exhausted with waiting for my God. . . .

Answer me, LORD, for your faithful love is good!
Turn to me in your great compassion! (Psalm 69:1-3, 16)

 Sit in silence and stillness for a few moments, lengthening the time each day if you are able.

Becoming Aware of God's Presence

Say to those who are panicking:
"Be strong! Don't fear!
Here's your God,
coming with vengeance;
with divine retribution
God will come to save you." (Isaiah 35:4)

Inviting God's Intervention

LORD, hear my prayer!
     Let my cry reach you!
Don't hide your face from me
     in my time of trouble!
Listen to me!
     Answer me quickly as I cry out! (Psalm 102:1-2)

Listening for God's Voice

Open yourself to hear what God is saying to you through the
Scriptures.

Be glad in the Lord always! Again I say, be glad! Let your
gentleness show in your treatment of all people. The Lord is near.
Don't be anxious about anything; rather, bring up all of your
requests to God in your prayers and petitions, along with giving
thanks. Then the peace of God that exceeds all understanding will
keep your hearts and minds safe in Christ Jesus.

From now on, brothers and sisters, if anything
is excellent and if anything is admirable, focus
your thoughts on these things: all that is true, all
that is holy, all that is just, all that is pure, all that
is lovely, and all that is worthy of praise. Practice
these things: whatever you learned, received,
heard, or saw in us. The God of peace will be
with you. (Philippians 4:4-9)

Alternative Readings

Deuteronomy 1:19-21
Luke 8:26-39
Joshua 24:14-15
Psalm 56
Matthew 8:23-27
Isaiah 12

Practicing Spiritual Reading

As you read the essay and one or more quotations each day, do so
with an openness for further contemplation on the week's theme. Ask
God, Is there a word or prayer for my life in these words?

We live in a fearful and anxious world. The constant bombardment
of 24-hour news reports reminding us again and again about disasters,
political infighting, threats from natural causes, and those branded as

enemies begins to penetrate our faith and trust in the God we have come to see most clearly in Jesus Christ. And as unnoticed as dusk turning to darkness, we easily and suddenly find ourselves in the darkness of fear and anxiety. Is there a way out of this darkness? Is there a way to "live in the light" of God's companionship that wipes away fear and anxiety as surely as the rising sun banishes the darkness of the night? The biblical witness is clear that the answer is, "Yes." And the lives of the saints who have gone before confirm that the biblical response to the question is true and transforming. When the frightened disciples awakened Jesus (Mark 4:38), he quickly calmed the sea and their fears. Today let us remind each other often that the resurrected Jesus no longer needs to be awakened but is a constant companion ready and able to calm our fears and walk with us through all the storms of life that come our way.

Jesus looks outward to the cosmos and to the sweep of human history before and after. He tells us we have no need to be anxious, for there is a divine life, the true home of the soul, that we can enter simply by placing our confidence in him: become his friend, and conspiring with him to subvert evil with good. He also shows us how we can be renewed in the depths of our soul, stepping "beyond the goodness of scribes and Pharisees" to become the kinds of persons who are genuinely at home in God's world. (Willard, *The Divine Conspiracy*, 215.)

As I began to see that darkness as something not to be feared but to be accepted and even embraced, I found others who had shared that experience. Few people talk about embracing the darkness. Far too often Christianity is seen as unending light; only those who have limited faith allow any darkness to creep in. But darkness is just as much a part of our lives as light. God made both the darkness and the light. By denying a place in our faith for darkness, we are limiting the ways in which we can encounter God. I know that my life and my faith have been richer because of the combination of light and darkness. Times of darkness contrast with times of joy, and it is that combination of light and dark that enriches our lives. (Soughers, *Treasures of Darkness*, 94.)

In careful observation of those who have demonstrated the capacity for faithful ministry characterized by a self-emptied heart and a life formed into the image of Christ, I have noted a consistent pattern in each of their lives. Their lives are marked with an unusual trust that permits them to act justly, love tenderly, and walk humbly with God (Micah 6:8).

In every case there is a simple trust in God. The words may be different but the theme is the same. God will provide. God's grace is adequate. (Job, *A Guide to Retreat*, 119.)

Taking Time to Reflect

 Pause and recall what you have read and heard, as well as your own life experiences. Take note of anything that particularly catches your attention—perhaps a word, phrase, or image.

Making Our Requests Known

Focus your prayers more specifically on particular things, persons, or circumstances. The following petitions offer guidance:

Prayers for God's Creation and Our World
Prayers for All God's People
Prayers for the Church and All Who Seek God
Prayers for Our Neighbors
Prayers for Our Families and Friends
Prayers for Ourselves

Thanking God for Our Prayers and Life

God of love, mercy, and peace,
pour out your Spirit upon us
to form and transform our lives
more and more into your
grand design for us all.
With trust and confidence,
we offer ourselves to you
and invite you to
bless and use us as you will,
for we are yours.

Prayer at the End of the Day

Inviting God's Activity

Tender Shepherd of my soul, make yourself and your way known to me in this evening time of prayer and reflection. By the power of your presence, bring me to the end of the day whole, complete, and at peace with you, my neighbor, and myself. Grant a night of peaceful rest and send me forth tomorrow as a witness to your love and grace.

A Continuing Request

Create a clean heart for me, God;
    put a new, faithful spirit deep inside me! (Psalm 51:10)

Gathering the Day

Remembering—Reflect on the day's experiences.

Confessing—Own up to your own weakness, failure, and sin.

Forgiving—Ask for and accept God's forgiveness, and forgive yourself and all who may have injured you or those you love.

Thanksgiving—Give thanks for the gifts that God has granted this day.

Offering

My whole being clings to you;
    your strong hand upholds me. (Psalm 63:8)

Blessing

I will lie down and fall asleep in peace
    because you alone, Lord, let me live in safety. (Psalm 4:8)

Week 35

Translating Good News into Good Actions

Approaching God with Intention

Holy God
  of unconditional love
  and unlimited presence,
  I come to make myself fully available
  to you, your will, and your way.
Speak to me gently and clearly,
  for I am yours
  and desire to hear, understand,
  and be obedient
  to your slightest whisper.
Speak, for I am listening.

 Sit in silence and stillness for a few moments, lengthening the time each day if you are able.

Becoming Aware of God's Presence

Lord, you are my God.
I will exalt you; I will praise your name,
  for you have done wonderful things,
    planned long ago, faithful and sure. (Isaiah 25:1)

Inviting God's Intervention

> I remember the days long past;
>> I meditate on all your deeds;
>> I contemplate your handiwork.
> I stretch out my hands to you;
>> my whole being is like dry dirt, thirsting for you.
>>> (Psalm 143:5-6)

Listening for God's Voice

Open yourself to hear what God is saying to you through the Scriptures.

> Brothers and sisters, we have confidence that we can enter the holy of holies by means of Jesus' blood, through a new and living way that he opened up for us through the curtain, which is his body, and we have a great high priest over God's house.
>
> Therefore, let's draw near with a genuine heart with the certainty that our faith gives us, since our hearts are sprinkled clean from an evil conscience and our bodies are washed with pure water.
>
> Let's hold on to the confession of our hope without wavering, because the one who made the promises is reliable.
>
> And let us consider each other carefully for the purpose of sparking love and good deeds. Don't stop meeting together with other believers, which some people have gotten into the habit of doing. Instead, encourage each other, especially as you see the day drawing near. (Hebrews 10:19-25)

Alternative Readings

2 Kings 2:1-2, 6-14
Hebrews 6:1-12
Matthew 10:40-42
Mark 5:21-43
Luke 9:51-62
Hebrews 10:32-39

Practicing Spiritual Reading

As you read the essay and one or more quotations each day, do so with an openness for further contemplation on the week's theme. Ask God, Is there a word or prayer for my life in these words?

Jesus spent his adult life doing good wherever he was. He seemed to be drawn to the needs and wounds of the world in which he lived his life. His life was truly the gospel; that is good news. The Gospel readings for this week are reflections of this way of life that left the world better, more whole, and more complete than he found it. It was a radical and risky way of living that is still transforming the world today.

Those who have heard the good news of the gospel and seek to follow Jesus as disciples are invited to live as Jesus did, translating the good news into holy action. It sounds so simple but can be highly challenging, because living the truth of the gospel requires living in fidelity with the gospel. Therefore we cannot ignore the needs of the world, or stand in judgment of those who are not like us. Rather we are compelled by integrity and love to attend to the needs of the world and stand in solidarity with all of God's children, even with those who are not like us. No matter how broken, bruised, confused, and lost, God stands with all, seeking to bring healing, hope, and ultimately bring all safely home. How can we this day translate the gospel into holy action that will join our lives to God's continuous action to transform the world? How will we translate "thy kingdom come, thy will be done" into a way of life?

When we see some of our ordinary activities as Christian practices, we come to perceive how *our daily lives are all tangled up with the things God is doing in the world.* . . . When we set ordinary daily activities in this context, they are transformed, and so are we. A meal becomes a time of forgiveness. An illness turns into an experience of solidarity with the poor. . . . A burial becomes a time of thanksgiving. (Craig Dykstra and Dorothy C. Bass, "Times of Yearning, Practices of Faith" in *Practicing Our Faith*, 8.)

Be bold enough to ask God to transform your own life and invest your life as leaven to transform the world where you are. Begin every day in seeking God's direction and companionship, and end every day in offering anew all you have done and all that you are to the One who gives you life. (Job, *A Wesleyan Spiritual Reader*, 194.)

Jesus walks into our daily lives in many ways—sometimes invited and sometimes not; sometimes welcome and sometimes not so welcome. But he always comes, the bearer of good news. Yet how often do our pre-conceived notions, our way of listening, prevent us from hearing him? (M. Basil Pennington, *Seeking His Mind: 40 Meetings with Christ*, 33.)

If Christ is born in our hearts, will the world ever feel it? Will government and business, our beloved earth or our disenfranchised masses be affected? We cannot answer that we are not good enough or are not schooled enough or are not recognized. We can only begin where we are. . . . To all those who receive him, who believe in his name, Christ still gives "the power to become the children of God" (John 1:12) and, with this inheritance, his grace to love to life the earth and all its people. (Grace Adolphsen Brame, *Faith, the Yes of the Heart*, 92.)

Taking Time to Reflect

Pause and recall what you have read and heard, as well as your own life experiences. Take note of anything that particularly catches your attention—perhaps a word, phrase, or image.

Making Our Requests Known

Focus your prayers more specifically on particular things, persons, or circumstances. The following petitions offer guidance:

Prayers for God's Creation and Our World
Prayers for All God's People
Prayers for the Church and All Who Seek God
Prayers for Our Neighbors
Prayers for Our Families and Friends
Prayers for Ourselves

Thanking God for Our Prayers and Life

Loving God,
I abandon my life into your care
with the assurance that you
will lead me in paths of righteousness
and goodness. Amen.

Prayer at the End of the Day

Inviting God's Activity

Tender Shepherd of my soul, make yourself and your way known to me in this evening time of prayer and reflection. By the power of your presence, bring me to the end of the day whole, complete, and at peace with you, my neighbor, and myself. Grant a night of peaceful rest and send me forth tomorrow as a witness to your love and grace.

A Continuing Request

Create a clean heart for me, God;
>   put a new, faithful spirit deep inside me! (Psalm 51:10)

Gathering the Day

Remembering—Reflect on the day's experiences.

Confessing—Own up to your own weakness, failure, and sin.

Forgiving—Ask for and accept God's forgiveness, and forgive yourself and all who may have injured you or those you love.

Thanksgiving—Give thanks for the gifts that God has granted this day.

Offering

My whole being clings to you;
>   your strong hand upholds me. (Psalm 63:8)

Blessing

I will lie down and fall asleep in peace
>   because you alone, LORD, let me live in safety. (Psalm 4:8)

Week 36

Chosen and Sent

Approaching God with Intention

O Divine Love, who calls and sends all who follow you, help me in this time apart to once more hear your voice. Grant grace to hear your voice calling and sending me, and grant faith enough to respond in obedience. Amen.

 Sit in silence and stillness for a few moments, lengthening the time each day if you are able.

Becoming Aware of God's Presence

Those who put their trust in the LORD,
    who pay no attention to the proud
    or to those who follow lies,
are truly happy! (Psalm 40:4)

Inviting God's Intervention

Favor me, LORD, and deliver me!
    LORD, come quickly and help me! (Psalm 40:13)

Listening for God's Voice

Open yourself to hear what God is saying to you through the Scriptures.

Jesus called the Twelve together and he gave them power and authority over all demons and to heal sicknesses. He sent them out to proclaim God's kingdom and to heal the sick. He told them, "Take nothing for the journey—no walking stick, no bag, no bread, no money, not even an extra shirt. Whatever house you enter, remain there until you leave that place. Wherever they don't welcome you, as you leave that city, shake the dust off your feet as a witness against them." They departed and went through the villages proclaiming the good news and healing people everywhere. (Luke 9:1-6)

Alternative Readings

Matthew 12:15-21

Luke 6:12-16

2 Kings 5:1-14

Psalm 30

Acts 6:1-6

Acts 16:6-10

Practicing Spiritual Reading

As you read the essay and one or more quotations each day, do so with an openness for further contemplation on the week's theme. Ask God, Is there a word or prayer for my life in these words?

Sometimes I forget that I did not think of God first, love God first, decide to follow God first, or even decide to permit myself to be sent by God. None of this was my idea at all. It all came from God. Even before I was made, God loved me and had already chosen me. How could I be so arrogant as to think it was my idea all along? Perhaps it was and is my desire to be in charge, to be in control of my own destiny, when deep within I know so very well that I am completely dependent upon God for all things.

I think those first disciples and I have at least that much in common. They were each sought out by God in Christ and had to be reminded who they were, who it was that gave them life and loved them without limit, and who it was that chose them and sent them to be witnesses to the world. Even after three years with Jesus, they needed each other and the power of the Holy Spirit to help them remember that they were indeed beloved, chosen, and sent into the world by God. I need as much today. How about you?

We are made in the image of God. We look at each person's journey beginning not with original sin but original grace. Our journeys all start and end with God, and everything we do is a step toward our return to wholeness. Because grace is our beginning, we are worthy of all good things. (The Women of Magdalene with Becca Stevens, *Find Your Way Home: Words from the Street, Wisdom from the Heart*, 19.)

You do not need to create the possibility of contact with the Spirit. In fact, you cannot create that possibility. For the Holy Spirit is all gift, entirely free. And the gift of the Holy Spirit is none other than the Holy Spirit. Knowing this, being grasped by this uninvited love, moves us to pray. The disciples pleaded with Jesus, "Lord teach us to pray," and Jesus has given us the Spirit to draw us into prayer, to guide us through prayer, to make up for our deficits in prayer, to pray on our behalf when we simply cannot pray. Our challenge is to stop erecting walls that separate us from the Spirit. (James C. Howell, *The Kiss of God: 27 Lessons on the Holy Spirit*, 27.)

A casual glimpse at the life of John Wesley may lead us to believe that life for him was without opposition. He knew where God was calling him to go, who God was calling him to be, and the rest was simple. . . .

The search for authentic discipleship led him to go far beyond the common understanding or practice of Christian faith, and this going beyond the commonly accepted way often led to opposition. . . .

The opposition he faced through all of life did not result in a gloomy attitude about life or the Christian faith. . . . He was able to see through the cross of life to the empty tomb. Opposition then became another gift from God to direct, form, and shape his journey of discipleship. (Rueben P. Job, *40 Days with Wesley: A Daily Devotional Journey*, 109–110.)

Taking Time to Reflect

Pause and recall what you have read and heard, as well as your own life experiences. Take note of anything that particularly catches your attention—perhaps a word, phrase, or image.

Making Our Requests Known

Focus your prayers more specifically on particular things, persons, or circumstances. The following petitions offer guidance:

Prayers for God's Creation and Our World
Prayers for All God's People
Prayers for the Church and All Who Seek God
Prayers for Our Neighbors
Prayers for Our Families and Friends
Prayers for Ourselves

Thanking God for Our Prayers and Life

Sustaining God,
in whom we find our identity and our life,
thank you for this time apart with you.
I offer to you all of my life
that I am able to give.
Accept and make holy
the gift of self that I bring
and send me from this place
renewed refreshed,
and redirected in your name. Amen.

Prayer at the End of the Day

Inviting God's Activity

Tender Shepherd of my soul, make yourself and your way known to me in this evening time of prayer and reflection. By the power of your presence, bring me to the end of the day whole, complete, and at peace with you, my neighbor, and myself. Grant a night of peaceful rest and send me forth tomorrow as a witness to your love and grace.

A Continuing Request

> Create a clean heart for me, God;
>> put a new, faithful spirit deep inside me! (Psalm 51:10)

Gathering the Day

Remembering—Reflect on the day's experiences.

Confessing—Own up to your own weakness, failure, and sin.

Forgiving—Ask for and accept God's forgiveness, and forgive yourself and all who may have injured you or those you love.

Thanksgiving—Give thanks for the gifts that God has granted this day.

Offering

> My whole being clings to you;
>> your strong hand upholds me. (Psalm 63:8)

Blessing

> I will lie down and fall asleep in peace
>> because you alone, LORD, let me live in safety. (Psalm 4:8)

Week 37

When Innocents Suffer

Approaching God with Intention

> Protect me from the power of the wicked, Lord!
>> Guard me from violent people
>>> who plot to trip me up!
> Arrogant people have laid a trap for me with ropes.
>> They've spread out a net alongside the road.
>> They've set snares for me. Selah
> I tell the Lord, "You are my God!
>> Listen to my request for mercy, Lord!" (Psalm 140:4-6)

 Sit in silence and stillness for a few moments, lengthening the time each day if you are able.

Becoming Aware of God's Presence

> But I wait for you, Lord!
>> You will answer, my Lord, my God! (Psalm 38:15)

Inviting God's Intervention

> Don't leave me all alone, Lord!
>> Please, my God, don't be far from me!
> Come quickly and help me,
>> my Lord, my salvation! (Psalm 38:21-22)

Listening for God's Voice

Open yourself to hear what God is saying to you through the Scriptures.

God takes his stand in the divine council;
    he gives judgment among the gods:
"How long will you judge unjustly
    by granting favor to the wicked? Selah
Give justice to the lowly and the orphan;
    maintain the right of the poor and the destitute!
Rescue the lowly and the needy.
    Deliver them from the power of the wicked!
They don't know; they don't understand;
    they wander around in the dark.
    All the earth's foundations shake. . . .

Rise up, God! Judge the earth
    because you hold all nations in your
    possession! (Psalm 82:1-5, 8)

Alternative Readings
Acts 7:54-60
Psalm 112
Acts 8:1-3
Luke 10:25-37
Job 21:1-16
Job 22

Practicing Spiritual Reading

As you read the essay and one or more quotations each day, do so with an openness for further contemplation on the week's theme. Ask God, Is there a word or prayer for my life in these words?

The Jesus movement was just getting started when it was shaken by the horrible execution of John the Baptist because of a political grudge. This is not the first or the last account of suffering that afflicted the innocent and the faithful. Soon the story of the Jesus movement includes the cruel execution of the Prince of Peace, Jesus, who was the most innocent and faithful of all. We need not look far in our world to see that the innocent still suffer and the faithful are still forsaken by the powers of the world that should defend and protect them.

Thanks be to God that is not the end of the story. For now as then, the darkness cannot put out the light, and now as then, there are those who will stand with and for the suffering innocents. And most of all the promises of God still prevail and our common prayer, "Thy Kingdom Come," is still being answered around the world as multitudes determine to love and serve God and neighbor, regardless of the cost. I want to be included in that community. How about you?

 Reconciliation must never become an isolated religious phenomenon, or sacramental practice, apart from the daily life of each of us. Just as sin involves multiple relationships, so does reconciliation. . . . Reconciliation involves both God and neighbors. Anyone committed to living a life of reconciliation must attend to the dynamics of love in relationship with God, others, self, and the world. (Gula, *To Walk Together Again*, 16.)

I love the simplicity of John's description of Jesus' appearance on that first Easter evening. (See John 20.) . . . The Risen Christ comes quietly and simply stands among his close group of followers. It's like the unobtrusive way he joined those despairing disciples on the road to Emmaus, quietly walking along with them so that they did not realize who he was (see Luke 24:13-35). You have to love the gentle patience of a resurrected Lord who shows up like that! In the upper room that night, Jesus spoke the words those fear-stricken disciples most deeply needed to hear, "Peace be with you" (John 20:19). Then he showed them the marks of the nails in his hands and feet, and the scar from the spear that had ripped open his side. Because of the scars, the disciples knew who he was. (James A. Harnish, *Strength for the Broken Places*, 17–18.)

Vaclav Havel said, "the salvation of this human world lies nowhere else than in the human heart." As we practice the disciplines of prayer and discernment, we seek not only personal salvation but also the salvation of the world that God created and loves. Havel's words are a reminder that we, too, have a part in the salvation of the world; our relationship with God is not only for our benefit but also for the benefit of the world. (Job, *Listen*, 8–9.)

Taking Time to Reflect

Pause and recall what you have read and heard, as well as your own life experiences. Take note of anything that particularly catches your attention—perhaps a word, phrase, or image.

Making Our Requests Known

Focus your prayers more specifically on particular things, persons, or circumstances. The following petitions offer guidance:

Prayers for God's Creation and Our World
Prayers for All God's People
Prayers for the Church and All Who Seek God
Prayers for Our Neighbors
Prayers for Our Families and Friends
Prayers for Ourselves

Thanking God for Our Prayers and Life

> I raise my eyes toward the mountains.
> > Where will my help come from?
> My help comes from the LORD,
> > the maker of heaven and earth. . . .
>
> The LORD is your protector;
> > the LORD is your shade right beside you.
> The sun won't strike you during the day;
> > neither will the moon at night.
> The LORD will protect you from all evil;
> > God will protect your very life. (Psalm 121:1-2, 5-7)

Prayer at the End of the Day

Inviting God's Activity

Tender Shepherd of my soul, make yourself and your way known to me in this evening time of prayer and reflection. By the power of your presence, bring me to the end of the day whole, complete, and at peace with you, my neighbor, and myself. Grant a night of peaceful rest and send me forth tomorrow as a witness to your love and grace.

A Continuing Request

Create a clean heart for me, God;
   put a new, faithful spirit deep inside me! (Psalm 51:10)

Gathering the Day

Remembering—Reflect on the day's experiences.

Confessing—Own up to your own weakness, failure, and sin.

Forgiving—Ask for and accept God's forgiveness, and forgive yourself and all who may have injured you or those you love.

Thanksgiving—Give thanks for the gifts that God has granted this day.

Offering

My whole being clings to you;
   your strong hand upholds me. (Psalm 63:8)

Blessing

I will lie down and fall asleep in peace
   because you alone, LORD, let me live in safety. (Psalm 4:8)

Week 38

Prayer, Compassion, and the Needs of the World

Approaching God with Intention

Loving Teacher, come and make your home in our hearts today. Teach us to do no harm, to do good, and assist us so that we may stay in loving relationship with you and our neighbors. Help us today to be an answer to another's prayer so that we may be one of your signs of hope in the world you love.

Sit in silence and stillness for a few moments, lengthening the time each day if you are able.

Becoming Aware of God's Presence

Open the gates of righteousness for me
    so I can come in and give thanks to the LORD!
This is the LORD's gate;
    those who are righteous enter through it.
I thank you because you answered me,
    because you were my saving help. (Psalm 118:19-21)

Inviting God's Intervention

> In tight circumstances, I cried out to the LORD.
>> The LORD answered me with wide-open spaces.
> The LORD is for me—I won't be afraid. (Psalm 118:5-6a)

Listening for God's Voice

Open yourself to hear what God is saying to you through the Scriptures.

> Now Jesus called his disciples and said, "I feel sorry for the crowd because they have been with me for three days and have nothing to eat. I don't want to send them away hungry for fear they won't have enough strength to travel."

> His disciples replied, "Where are we going to get enough food in this wilderness to satisfy such a big crowd?"

> Jesus said, "How much bread do you have?" They responded, "Seven loaves and a few fish."

> He told the crowd to sit on the ground. He took the seven loaves of bread and the fish. After he gave thanks, he broke them into pieces and gave them to the disciples, and the disciples gave them to the crowds. Everyone ate until they were full. The disciples collected seven baskets full of leftovers. Four thousand men ate, plus women and children. After dismissing the crowds, Jesus got into the boat and came to the region of Magadan. (Matthew 15:32-39)

Alternative Readings

Mark 6:30-34, 53-56
Colossians 1:15-28
Psalm 111
Matthew 9:35-38
Isaiah 55:1-3
Romans 12:9-13

Practicing Spiritual Reading

As you read the essay and one or more quotations each day, do so with an openness for further contemplation on the week's theme. Ask God, Is there a word or prayer for my life in these words?

Returning from the mission upon which Jesus had sent them, the disciples were filled with a success story that would make anyone proud and pleased. They poured out their story to Jesus, and while he recognized their elation, he also recognized their exhaustion and said, "Come away to a deserted place all by yourselves and rest a while" (Mark 6:31 NRSV). We have all experienced the emotional, physical, and spiritual exhaustion that follows an intense giving of ourselves to a cause greater than we are. Left unattended this exhaustion can be extremely debilitating. So Jesus immediately took the disciples on a retreat. Their boat trip to the place of solitude was a necessary, healing, and life-giving move on the part of Jesus. But once there, the compassion of Jesus led him to respond to the needs of the gathered crowd and for the moment to forget the weariness that he and his disciples were carrying. And once again he was teaching and healing as he asked the disciples to give the crowd something to eat.

Prayer, compassion, and the needs of the world are always woven into any faithful life of discipleship. If we are wise, we will weave them into a beautiful way of living that brings healing and hope to the world and fulfillment, joy, and peace to ourselves. At this point, a word of caution is in order. Jesus had the wisdom to know when time apart was essential and when it was wise to once again engage in ministry. He was clear about resources and about limits. Once again, this is where we as followers must seek and follow the leading and direction that God seeks to bestow.

"The time of business," said he, "does not with me differ from the time of prayer; and in the noise and clatter of my kitchen, while several persons are at the same time calling for different things, I possess GOD in as great tranquility as if I were upon my knees at the blessed sacrament." (Brother Lawrence, *The Practice of the Presence of God*, 25.)

It is this loving, steadfast, unshakable God who hovered over all creation and declared that it was very good (Genesis 1:31). This same God, revealed in Jesus, calls all to come home and intentionally dwell in God's presence. It is this God who chooses to move all that is toward justice, peace, harmony, and plenty—not just for a few, but for all. In Jesus we see a God who is moving all things toward the kingdom of righteousness, the kingdom of God. (Job, *Three Simple Questions*, 26–27.)

Jesus' organization was loose and fluid; the most prominent characteristic of the organization was that it didn't have one! . . . Rather than devote most of his time to administering an organization as our secular world understands it, Jesus spent his time revealing the kingdom of God from within the situations he encountered. If he needed to feed the people, he created a food program (John 6:1-14); if healing was needed, any place could become a clinic (Mark 6:53-56); if teaching was necessary, the world was the classroom (Matt. 5); finally, if a parade was required, a colt or donkey could be borrowed (Matt. 21:2). And just as quickly, all these "organizations" could disappear when they were no longer necessary. (Daniel Wolpert, *Leading a Life With God: The Practice of Spiritual Leadership*, 141.)

Taking Time to Reflect

Pause and recall what you have read and heard, as well as your own life experiences. Take note of anything that particularly catches your attention—perhaps a word, phrase, or image.

Making Our Requests Known

Focus your prayers more specifically on particular things, persons, or circumstances. The following petitions offer guidance:

Prayers for God's Creation and Our World
Prayers for All God's People
Prayers for the Church and All Who Seek God
Prayers for Our Neighbors
Prayers for Our Families and Friends
Prayers for Ourselves

Thanking God for Our Prayers and Life

Grant to me, O God,
The continual guidance, strength,
And help of your Holy Spirit
So that I may serve faithfully
In your world.
Grant me grace to live
In such a way
As to please you
And reflect your presence to others.
In the name of Christ. Amen.

Prayer at the End of the Day

Inviting God's Activity

Tender Shepherd of my soul, make yourself and your way known to me in this evening time of prayer and reflection. By the power of your presence, bring me to the end of the day whole, complete, and at peace with you, my neighbor, and myself. Grant a night of peaceful rest and send me forth tomorrow as a witness to your love and grace.

A Continuing Request

Create a clean heart for me, God;
    put a new, faithful spirit deep inside me! (Psalm 51:10)

Gathering the Day

Remembering—Reflect on the day's experiences.

Confessing—Own up to your own weakness, failure, and sin.

Forgiving—Ask for and accept God's forgiveness, and forgive yourself and all who may have injured you or those you love.

Thanksgiving—Give thanks for the gifts that God has granted this day.

Offering

My whole being clings to you;
    your strong hand upholds me. (Psalm 63:8)

Blessing

I will lie down and fall asleep in peace
    because you alone, LORD, let me live in safety. (Psalm 4:8)

Prayer Practice

Intentional Listening and Journaling

Learning to live in communion with Jesus Christ is a lifelong experience. Learning to listen intently for God's message to you in Scripture, story, the events of the day, and your times of silence and prayer will open your mind and heart to the best ways for you to access and receive the mentoring of God.

One tool that can help you learn to listen with intent is note-taking. As you read a Scripture passage today or any day, be even more intentional in your reflection and meditation on the reading. Spend more time listening for and recording the urgings, cautions, and encouragements of the Holy Spirit, as well as the specific actions you are prompted to take.

If you desire, consider expanding your note-taking to more in-depth journaling. Use a separate notebook or journal. Write out your prayers and what you hear God saying to you. Note specific petitions and answers to prayer. Over time, a prayer journal can help you to see how God is speaking and working in your life.

(Job, *Listen*, 54.)

Week 39

Teach Us to Pray

Approaching God with Intention

Loving God,
Who understands before I form my prayer,
Who hears when I call and translates my humble words
    into beautiful hymns of gratitude and praise
And responds to my uncertain cry for help
    with assurance, peace, and palpable presence,
Here I am as fully in your presence
    as I am able to be,
Offering my fears, my needs, my hopes,
    my love, and my life,
For I am yours and belong to no other.

 Sit in silence and stillness for a few moments, lengthening the time each day if you are able.

Becoming Aware of God's Presence

> But let all who seek you
>   celebrate and rejoice in you.
> Let those who love your salvation always say,
>   "The Lᴏʀᴅ is great!"
> But me? I'm weak and needy.

Let my Lord think of me.
You are my help and my rescuer.
> My God, don't wait any longer! (Psalm 40:16-17)

Inviting God's Intervention

Just like a deer that craves streams of water,
> my whole being craves you, God.
My whole being thirsts for God, for the living God.
> When will I come and see God's face? (Psalm 42:1-2)

Listening for God's Voice

Open yourself to hear what God is saying to you through the Scriptures.

Jesus was telling them a parable about their need to pray continuously and not to be discouraged. He said, "In a certain city there was a judge who neither feared God nor respected people. In that city there was a widow who kept coming to him, asking, 'Give me justice in this case against my adversary.' For a while he refused but finally said to himself, I don't fear God or respect people, but I will give this widow justice because she keeps bothering me. Otherwise, there will be no end to her coming here and embarrassing me." The Lord said, "Listen to what the unjust judge says. Won't God provide justice to his chosen people who cry out to him day and night? Will he be slow to help them? I tell you, he will give them justice quickly. But when the Human One comes, will he find faithfulness on earth?"
(Luke 18:1-8)

Alternative Readings

Matthew 7:7-11
Mark 11:20-25
Psalm 141:1-5
Isaiah 56:6-8
2 Corinthians 3:1-6
1 John 3:18-24

Practicing Spiritual Reading

As you read the essay and one or more quotations each day, do so with an openness for further contemplation on the week's theme. Ask God, Is there a word or prayer for my life in these words?

Three years of face-to-face, in-the-flesh time with Jesus, and it appears that the disciples asked him to teach them only one thing. They must have known there was much they did not know about being a disciple and bearing witness to the gospel. And yet, they asked Jesus to teach them just one thing: how to pray. Was it because it was such a difficult thing to learn how to pray? Or, was it that they saw it was the essential practice, the center of power, the ultimate source of companionship, the connection to the loving Abba that Jesus loved, listened to, and obeyed? I believe it was the latter, and the disciples wanted what Jesus had and wanted to be like Jesus and wanted to live like Jesus. And they could see that there was only one way to receive that gift, and it was through prayer. So the one thing they asked Jesus to teach them was to pray. Jesus promised the Spirit would teach us everything we need to know (John 14:26), and Paul confirms the Spirit's assistance as we pray (Romans 8:26). And so today we pray the prayer Jesus taught us and try to follow its themes in our own prayers and still we ask, as did those first disciples, "Teach us to pray." Because we too want to stay connected to our divine Abba and live as Jesus lived.

Whatever else it may be, prayer is first and foremost an act of love. . . . Jesus prayed primarily because he loved his Father. . . . His personal experience of Yahweh Sabaoth as loving Father shaped not only his self-understanding but, like a knife slashing through wallpaper, brought a dramatic breakthrough into undreamed-of intimacy with God in prayer. Childlike candor, boundless trust, easy familiarity, deep reverence, joyful dependence, unflagging obedience, unmistakable tenderness, and an innate sense of belonging characterized Jesus' prayer. (Brennan Manning, *A Glimpse of Jesus: The Stranger to Self-Hatred*, 83–84.)

I have a friend who describes his life of prayer as "staying in touch with the home office." I have other friends who describe their prayer lives as mostly verbal or mostly reading and responding to Scripture, others who seek ways to fulfill the biblical call to "pray without ceasing" (1 Thessalonians 5:17 NRSV), and still others who make the ancient liturgy and prayers of the church their own. And yet, within all of this diversity there is a unifying constant. That unifying constant is a movement toward God that results in transformation of life and how life is valued and lived out in the everyday experiences of our existence. (Job, *Three Simple Rules*, 66.)

To live without prayer is to live without God, to live without a soul. (Abraham J. Heschel, *Between God and Man: An Interpretation of Judaism*, 211.)

Prayer is not meant to be complicated, complex, and left to professionals. Prayer is for all of us. It is simply offering the fears, needs, hopes, longings, and questions of our minds and hearts to God as honestly, earnestly, and accurately as we can. Our prayers also express the essence of who we are and what our relationship is with God. Yet it is not our initiative that begins our prayer. Rather, it is God's seeking love and invitation that awaken within us the desire, courage, and need to pray. (Job, *Listen*, 51.)

Taking Time to Reflect

 Pause and recall what you have read and heard, as well as your own life experiences. Take note of anything that particularly catches your attention—perhaps a word, phrase, or image.

Making Our Requests Known

Focus your prayers more specifically on particular things, persons, or circumstances. The following petitions offer guidance:

Prayers for God's Creation and Our World
Prayers for All God's People
Prayers for the Church and All Who Seek God
Prayers for Our Neighbors
Prayers for Our Families and Friends
Prayers for Ourselves

Thanking God for Our Prayers and Life

> I hope, LORD.
> My whole being hopes,
>   and I wait for God's promise.
> My whole being waits for my Lord —
>   more than the night watch waits for morning;
>   yes, more than the night watch waits for morning!
>   (Psalm 130:5-6)

Prayer at the End of the Day

Inviting God's Activity

Tender Shepherd of my soul, make yourself and your way known to me in this evening time of prayer and reflection. By the power of your presence, bring me to the end of the day whole, complete, and at peace with you, my neighbor, and myself. Grant a night of peaceful rest and send me forth tomorrow as a witness to your love and grace.

A Continuing Request

Create a clean heart for me, God;
    put a new, faithful spirit deep inside me! (Psalm 51:10)

Gathering the Day

Remembering—Reflect on the day's experiences.

Confessing—Own up to your own weakness, failure, and sin.

Forgiving—Ask for and accept God's forgiveness, and forgive yourself and all who may have injured you or those you love.

Thanksgiving—Give thanks for the gifts that God has granted this day.

Offering

My whole being clings to you;
    your strong hand upholds me. (Psalm 63:8)

Blessing

I will lie down and fall asleep in peace
    because you alone, LORD, let me live in safety. (Psalm 4:8)

Week 40

Guarding Against Greed

Approaching God with Intention

O God of Mercy, make yourself known to me. Illumine and remove from my life those sins and distractions that prevent me from being attentive and faithful. Grant to me faith, wisdom, and courage to see and rejoice in your promises for my future. Amen.

 Sit in silence and stillness for a few moments, lengthening the time each day if you are able.

Becoming Aware of God's Presence

Heaven is declaring God's glory;
    the sky is proclaiming his handiwork.
One day gushes the news to the next,
    and one night informs another what needs to be known.
Of course, there's no speech, no words—
      their voices can't be heard—
but their sound extends throughout the world;
      their words reach the ends of the earth. (Psalm 19:1-4)

Inviting God's Intervention

Send your light and truth—those will guide me!
    Let them bring me to your holy mountain,
      to your dwelling place. (Psalm 43:3)

Listening for God's Voice

Open yourself to hear what God is saying to you through the Scriptures.

Tell people who are rich at this time not to become egotistical and not to place their hope on their finances, which are uncertain. Instead, they need to hope in God, who richly provides everything for our enjoyment. Tell them to do good, to be rich in the good things they do, to be generous, and to share with others. When they do these things, they will save a treasure for themselves that is a good foundation for the future. That way they can take hold of what is truly life. (1 Timothy 6:17-19)

Alternative Readings

Matthew 19:16-22
Matthew 19:27-30
Jeremiah 6:13-16
2 Peter 2:1-3
Matthew 20:1-26
Psalm 17:1-7, 15.

Practicing Spiritual Reading

As you read the essay and one or more quotations each day, do so with an openness for further contemplation on the week's theme. Ask God, Is there a word or prayer for my life in these words?

In John 14:23, Jesus reminds us that we are invited to become a holy chalice in which God chooses to dwell: "Whoever loves me will keep my word. My Father will love them, and we will come to them and make our home with them." Even before we are fully aware of this truth, we are already claimed as children of God. We were made in God's image, and God chooses to dwell within us.

When each of us claims our full inheritance as a child of God, we see clearly that we are given this wonderful world to tend and to share as God's family. In the eyes of Jesus, we are not given a special place because of our birth, place of origin, wealth, gender, or occupation. As children of God, all receive an identity and place as God's beloved child. And those who choose to serve receive honorable mention. "Jesus called them over and said, 'You know that those who rule the Gentiles show off their authority over them and their high-ranking officials order them around. But that's not the way it will be with you.

Whoever wants to be great among you will be your servant'" (Matthew 20:25-26). Serving others is following the way of love, justice, and truth. (Job, *Three Simple Questions*, 41–42.)

 One of the wonders of the world is the rampant sin that flourishes to applause in Christian communities and organizations. Ambition and pride and avarice are uncritically given places of honor and then "supported" with a proof text and sealed with prayer. Jesus is not an uncritical prayer-answerer. He has been through this before. Those forty days and nights of desert temptation allowed no room for naiveté in these matters. Everything that the devil put before Jesus was wrapped in Scripture packaging. Jesus was not tempted by the obvious evil but by the apparent good. He saw through it and stood fast. And now he sees through this man's so very correct prayer—and stands fast. . . . (Luke 12:13-21) (Peterson, *Tell It Slant*, 58–59.)

The journey of discovering what we're born for seems first to lead us to death. That is not a hopeless place, though. I suspect from it will emerge some clue about what—or whom—we'd be willing to die for. For from the cold stone of a threatened life we instinctively venture back to the fire, the one that warms us and keeps our blood moving. (Jo Kadlecek, *Woman Overboard: How Passion Saved My Life*, 79.)

Those who have gone before us along the pathway of discernment, seeking only God's will and way, remind us that dissatisfaction with things as they are is one essential element in discovering God's will. When we are settled and very comfortable, it is hard to listen for and respond to God's voice calling us to move out, over, up, beyond, or even to new ministry where we are. (Job, *A Guide to Spiritual Discernment*, 36.)

Almighty and everlasting GOD, the sovereign LORD of all creatures in heaven and earth, we acknowledge that our being, and all the comforts of it, depend on thee, the fountain of all good. We have nothing but what is owing entirely to thy free and bounteous love, O most blessed Creator, and to the riches of thy grace, O most blessed Redeemer. (John Wesley, *A Collection of Prayers for Families*, na.)

Taking Time to Reflect

 Pause and recall what you have read and heard, as well as your own life experiences. Take note of anything that particularly catches your attention—perhaps a word, phrase, or image.

Making Our Requests Known

Focus your prayers more specifically on particular things, persons, or circumstances. The following petitions offer guidance:

Prayers for God's Creation and Our World
Prayers for All God's People
Prayers for the Church and All Who Seek God
Prayers for Our Neighbors
Prayers for Our Families and Friends
Prayers for Ourselves

Thanking God for Our Prayers and Life

Giver of every good and perfect gift,
accept the offering I make
and lead me in paths of goodness
and truth.
Deliver me from the false impression
that I can follow you, love as you did,
and live on my own strength.
Guide me in forgiveness and new life.
Amen.

Prayer at the End of the Day

Inviting God's Activity

Tender Shepherd of my soul, make yourself and your way known to me in this evening time of prayer and reflection. By the power of your presence, bring me to the end of the day whole, complete, and at peace with you, my neighbor, and myself. Grant a night of peaceful rest and send me forth tomorrow as a witness to your love and grace.

A Continuing Request

Create a clean heart for me, God;
   put a new, faithful spirit deep inside me! (Psalm 51:10)

Gathering the Day

Remembering—Reflect on the day's experiences.

Confessing—Own up to your own weakness, failure, and sin.

Forgiving—Ask for and accept God's forgiveness, and forgive yourself and all who may have injured you or those you love.

Thanksgiving—Give thanks for the gifts that God has granted this day.

Offering

My whole being clings to you;
   your strong hand upholds me. (Psalm 63:8)

Blessing

I will lie down and fall asleep in peace
   because you alone, Lord, let me live in safety. (Psalm 4:8)

Week 41

God's Pleasure

Approaching God with Intention

Holy God,
Speak to me gently and clearly
    for I am yours
    and desire to hear, understand,
    and be obedient
    to your slightest whisper.
Amen.

 Sit in silence and stillness for a few moments, lengthening the time each day if you are able.

Becoming Aware of God's Presence

The truly happy person
        doesn't follow wicked advice,
        doesn't stand on the road of sinners,
        and doesn't sit with the disrespectful.
Instead of doing those things,
        these persons love the LORD's Instruction,
        and they recite God's Instruction day and night!
                                        (Psalm 1:1-2)

Inviting God's Intervention

Why do you stand so far away, LORD,
    hiding yourself in troubling times?
Meanwhile, the wicked are proudly
    in hot pursuit of those who suffer.
Let them get caught
    in the very same schemes they've thought up! (Psalm 10:1-2)

Listening for God's Voice

Open yourself to hear what God is saying to you through the Scriptures.

I cry out to you from the depths, LORD—
my Lord, listen to my voice!
    Let your ears pay close attention to my request for mercy!
If you kept track of sins, LORD—
    my Lord, who would stand a chance?
But forgiveness is with you—
    that's why you are honored.

I hope, LORD.
My whole being hopes,
    and I wait for God's promise.
My whole being waits for my Lord —
    more than the night watch waits for
    morning;
    yes, more than the night watch waits for
    morning! (Psalm 130:1-6)

Alternative Readings

Matthew 6:25-33
Romans 14:13-23
Matthew 3:1-6
Galatians 4:1-7
Ephesians 2:1-10
1 Peter 4:7-11

Practicing Spiritual Reading

As you read the essay and one or more quotations each day, do so with an openness for further contemplation on the week's theme. Ask God, Is there a word or prayer for my life in these words?

Taking appropriate care of self and living selflessly are not opposites. Rather they are each essential elements of a healthy and productive life. To love God with all of life and to love neighbor as self is not to denigrate, deny, or devalue self. It is to proclaim the heart of our theology as Christians and to place enormous value on self and on neighbor. It is to choose to live in the reign of God NOW. To begin to live as a citizen of a new order in which God's love for all creation is recognized and proclaimed in word and deed. . . .

Loving oneself does demand caring for oneself in a culture and in systems that are often destructive to self. And that self-care begins with the acknowledgement and reminder that each one of us is the object of God's love. Each one of us is embraced in the unlimited, saving, and transforming love of God. Each one of us is the "apple of [God's] eye" and is always and ultimately safe in the strong arms of God (Zechariah 2:8). When this knowledge is deeply imbedded within, we are better able to see the distinction between denying self and caring for self. (Job, *Three Simple Rules*, 46–47.)

 Here is the God I want to believe in: a Father who, from the beginning of creation, has stretched out his arms in merciful blessing, never forcing himself on anyone, but always waiting; never letting his arms drop down in despair, but always hoping that his children will return so that he can speak words of love to them and let his tired arms rest on their shoulders. His only desire is to bless. (Henri J. M. Nouwen, *The Return of the Prodigal Son: A Story of Homecoming*, 93–94.)

Until I become truly aware of the world in which I live, I cannot possibly get more out of a situation than a mere outline of reality, a kind of caricature of time. It takes a lifetime to really understand that God is in what is standing in front of me. Most of life is spent looking, straining to see the God in the mist, behind the cloud, beyond the dark. It is when we face God in one another, in creation, in the moment, that the real spiritual journey begins. Everything in life is meant to stretch me beyond my superficial self to my better self, to the Ultimate Good who is God. But before that can happen, I must be alive in it myself. I must ask of everything in life: What is this saying to me about life? (Joan Chittister, *Illuminated Life: Monastic Wisdom for Seekers of Light*, 24.)

No Christian should live with the weight of unforgiven sin and unresolved guilt. The assurance that we are forgiven, that we can begin again with a new page of life upon which to write our story, is the gift of God's justifying grace for all. But this is not the end of our relationship with God, the end of faith, or the end of our journey toward righteousness. Rather, it is the beginning of a quest for a life of goodness and holiness. (Job, *40 Days With Wesley*, 97.)

Taking Time to Reflect

 Pause and recall what you have read and heard, as well as your own life experiences. Take note of anything that particularly catches your attention—perhaps a word, phrase, or image.

Making Our Requests Known

Focus your prayers more specifically on particular things, persons, or circumstances. The following petitions offer guidance:

Prayers for God's Creation and Our World
Prayers for All God's People
Prayers for the Church and All Who Seek God
Prayers for Our Neighbors
Prayers for Our Families and Friends
Prayers for Ourselves

Thanking God for Our Prayers and Life

> LORD, you have examined me.
>> You know me. . . .
>
> You are the one who created my innermost parts;
>> you knit me together while I was still in my mother's womb.
> I give thanks to you that I was marvelously set apart.
>> Your works are wonderful—I know that very well.
>
> God, your plans are incomprehensible to me!
>> Their total number is countless!
> If I tried to count them—they outnumber grains of sand!
>> If I came to the very end—I'd still be with you.
>>> (Psalm 139: 1, 13-14, 17-18)

Prayer at the End of the Day

Inviting God's Activity

Tender Shepherd of my soul, make yourself and your way known to me in this evening time of prayer and reflection. By the power of your presence, bring me to the end of the day whole, complete, and at peace with you, my neighbor, and myself. Grant a night of peaceful rest and send me forth tomorrow as a witness to your love and grace.

A Continuing Request

Create a clean heart for me, God;
> put a new, faithful spirit deep inside me! (Psalm 51:10)

Gathering the Day

Remembering—Reflect on the day's experiences.

Confessing—Own up to your own weakness, failure, and sin.

Forgiving—Ask for and accept God's forgiveness, and forgive yourself and all who may have injured you or those you love.

Thanksgiving—Give thanks for the gifts that God has granted this day.

Offering

My whole being clings to you;
> your strong hand upholds me. (Psalm 63:8)

Blessing

I will lie down and fall asleep in peace
> because you alone, Lord, let me live in safety. (Psalm 4:8)

Week 42

Love Trumps Division

Approaching God with Intention

Tender Shepherd,
Gather us together as your flock,
Defend us from division,
Save us from sin,
Lead us in paths of righteousness, justice, peace,
    unity, and love,
Help us to discern wisely and well your will and
    way,
And grant us grace to follow faithfully. Amen.

 Sit in silence and stillness for a few moments, lengthening the time each day if you are able.

Becoming Aware of God's Presence

Who can live in your tent, LORD?
    Who can dwell on your holy mountain?
The person who
    lives free of blame,
    does what is right,
        and speaks the truth sincerely;
    who does no damage with their talk,

does no harm to a friend,
doesn't insult a neighbor. (Psalm 15:1-3)

Inviting God's Intervention

Get up, LORD!
Get your fist ready, God!
Don't forget the ones who suffer!
Why do the wicked reject God?
Why do they think to themselves
that you won't find out? (Psalm 10:12-13)

Listening for God's Voice

Open yourself to hear what God is saying to you through the Scriptures.

"You have heard that it was said, You must love your neighbor and hate your enemy. But I say to you, love your enemies and pray for those who harass you so that you will be acting as children of your Father who is in heaven. He makes the sun rise on both the evil and the good and sends rain on both the righteous and the unrighteous. If you love only those who love you, what reward do you have? Don't even the tax collectors do the same? And if you greet only your brothers and sisters, what more are you doing? Don't even the Gentiles do the same? Therefore, just as your heavenly Father is complete in showing love to everyone, so also you must be complete.
(Matthew 5:43-48)

Alternative Readings

John 7:40-44
Micah 7:1-7
1 Corinthians 4:8-13
Psalm 133
Romans 8:35-39
Luke 6:27-36

Practicing Spiritual Reading

As you read the essay and one or more quotations each day, do so with an openness for further contemplation on the week's theme. Ask God, Is there a word or prayer for my life in these words?

We live in a divisive and violent world. While division, conflict, and violence are as old as Genesis, they are also as new and troubling as the current religious conflicts and the latest violence of word and act. There is near universal agreement that the way of division and violence is destructive and can never usher in the Kingdom for which Jesus taught us to pray. And yet we seem unable to incorporate the full range of Jesus' teaching about the futility of any other way than the way of love. Jesus was clear that his message and he himself would push individuals to decide and choose whom they would follow. But his message was clear: Love always trumps violence and division. For love always draws us toward one another and toward God, and violence always separates us and moves us away from God as we move away from the chosen way of life that Jesus modeled and taught.

In my better moments I always want to bring reconciliation, unity, and peace to every community of which I am a part. And when I become too frightened by the risk of doing so I remember that Jesus demonstrated that love always trumps violence and division. So I pray for grace to always play the trump card God has given.

 Jesus called his disciples to the impossible: "Love your enemies; do good to those who hate you; speak well of those who speak evil of you; pray for those who persecute you." (Luke 6) Yes, this is the impossible love that Jesus comes to announce in order that humanity work towards unity. This way of non-violence, forgiveness, and reconciliation, of acceptance of people who are different . . . will shake all the foundations of societies closed in upon themselves. . . . This transformation will take time, for the Kingdom grows little by little like a seed; it is founded on love and on communion. (Jean Vanier, *Jesus, the Gift of Love*, 96–97.)

Perhaps the most essential characteristic of our spiritual life is expressed in offering one another unconditional acceptance as persons. . . . When we stand firmly on the ground of unconditional acceptance, mutual commitment, and encouragement, we are in a position to confront one another with needed challenges out of a posture of love. Paul calls this spiritual art "speaking the truth in love" (Eph. 4:15). It is truly a demanding skill, beginning with the discipline of discerning what is true and following with the capacity both to offer authentic appreciation when fitting and to confront gently yet firmly when needed. . . . The deceptively simple phrase, "speaking the truth in love," clearly indicates that the *spirit* in which one speaks truth is as important as the truth one speaks. (Marjorie J. Thompson, *Family: The Forming Center*, 59, 61.)

When Paul spoke of Christ making the two of us one, he spoke of only the world he knew: one divided into Jesus and Gentiles. He could not have known the full import of his words. Jesus came to break down the barriers that separate all peoples, not just Jews and Gentiles. He is the one who comes to reconcile the First World with the Second World and the Third World. Paul could never have expressed it in that way; even you and I could not have expressed it that way even a few decades ago. (William H. Shannon, *Seeds of Peace: Contemplation and Non-Violence*, 108–109.)

Taking Time to Reflect

Pause and recall what you have read and heard, as well as your own life experiences. Take note of anything that particularly catches your attention—perhaps a word, phrase, or image.

Making Our Requests Known

Focus your prayers more specifically on particular things, persons, or circumstances. The following petitions offer guidance:

Prayers for God's Creation and Our World
Prayers for All God's People
Prayers for the Church and All Who Seek God
Prayers for Our Neighbors
Prayers for Our Families and Friends
Prayers for Ourselves

Thanking God for Our Prayers and Life

Holy God
of unconditional love
and unlimited presence,
I come to make myself fully available
to you, your will, and your way. Amen.

Prayer at the End of the Day

Inviting God's Activity

Tender Shepherd of my soul, make yourself and your way known to me in this evening time of prayer and reflection. By the power of your presence, bring me to the end of the day whole, complete, and at peace with you, my neighbor, and myself. Grant a night of peaceful rest and send me forth tomorrow as a witness to your love and grace.

A Continuing Request

Create a clean heart for me, God;
    put a new, faithful spirit deep inside me! (Psalm 51:10)

Gathering the Day

Remembering—Reflect on the day's experiences.

Confessing—Own up to your own weakness, failure, and sin.

Forgiving—Ask for and accept God's forgiveness, and forgive yourself and all who may have injured you or those you love.

Thanksgiving—Give thanks for the gifts that God has granted this day.

Offering

My whole being clings to you;
    your strong hand upholds me. (Psalm 63:8)

Blessing

I will lie down and fall asleep in peace
    because you alone, LORD, let me live in safety. (Psalm 4:8)

Week 43

Whom Shall We Follow?

Approaching God with Intention

Lord God of heavenly forces,
  hear my prayer;
  listen closely, Jacob's God! (Psalm 84:8)

 Sit in silence and stillness for a few moments, lengthening the time each day if you are able.

Becoming Aware of God's Presence

How lovely is your dwelling place,
  Lord of heavenly forces!
My very being longs, even yearns,
  for the Lord's courtyards.
My heart and my body
  will rejoice out loud to the living God! (Psalm 84:1-2)

Inviting God's Intervention

Look at our shield, God;
  pay close attention to the face of your anointed one!
Better is a single day in your courtyards
  than a thousand days anywhere else! (Psalm 84:9-10a)

Listening for God's Voice

Open yourself to hear what God is saying to you through the Scriptures.

> The time came for the Festival of Dedication in Jerusalem. It was winter, and Jesus was in the temple, walking in the covered porch named for Solomon. The Jewish opposition circled around him and asked, "How long will you test our patience? If you are the Christ, tell us plainly."

> Jesus answered, "I have told you, but you don't believe. The works I do in my Father's name testify about me, but you don't believe because you don't belong to my sheep. My sheep listen to my voice. I know them and they follow me. I give them eternal life. They will never die, and no one will snatch them from my hand. My Father, who has given them to me, is greater than all, and no one is able to snatch them from my Father's hand. I and the Father are one." (John 10:22-30)

Alternative Readings

Luke 9:57-62
Psalm 71:1-6
Matthew 8:18-22
1 John 2:26-29
1 John 3:1-4
John 10:1-4

Practicing Spiritual Reading

As you read the essay and one or more quotations each day, do so with an openness for further contemplation on the week's theme. Ask God, Is there a word or prayer for my life in these words?

Many people were offended. They just could not believe what Jesus was saying. "It is the spirit that gives life; the flesh is useless. The words I have spoken to you are spirit and life" (John 6:63 NRSV). As quickly as they turned toward Jesus, they now turned away. Because so many turned away, Jesus turned to the Twelve and gave them opportunity to go with the crowd. "Do you also wish to go away?" Jesus asked (verse 67 NRSV). He was very aware of the pressure that culture, country, and religion were exerting on all who lived in such a troubled time and place. So now the chosen ones are given the opportunity to make their own choice. As you might expect, Peter was the first to speak. "Lord, to whom can we go? You have the words of eternal life. We have come to believe and know that you are the Holy One of God" (6:68b-69 NRSV). After watching the crowd walk away, and considering the options, they chose to follow Jesus.

Many are still offended today by the company Jesus keeps, by the words he speaks and the invitation he continually gives to follow up close and to become as engaged with life in this troubled time and place as he is. And very likely we will have opportunity every day to choose to follow Jesus or turn away in offense or fear. I am praying for grace and strength to respond something like Peter did.

 Consider it like this. You have offered yourselves, one way or another, to try to work for God. You want, as it were, to be one among the sheepdogs employed by the Good Shepherd. Now have you ever watched a good sheepdog at his work? He is not at all an emotional animal. He just goes on with his job quite steadily, takes no notice of bad weather, rough ground, or his own comfort. He seldom or never comes back to be stroked. Yet his faithfulness, his intimate understanding with his master, is one of the loveliest things in the world. Now and then he just looks at the shepherd. When the time comes for rest they can generally be found together. Let this be the model of our love. (Underhill, *The Ways of the Spirit*, 62.)

The prayer practice known as THE EXAMEN helps us to see the will of God in action. . . . The examen asks us to look back over a period of time or review an event, looking for glimmers, moments, and actions that appear to be either "of God" or not "of God." The former are the life-giving things that bring the fruits of the Spirit, while the latter are those things that are death-dealing and bring fruits of a spirit that is not God. . . . The prayerful *examen*-ation of the past helps us in our discernment of the future because we begin to see the trajectory of God's action in our place and our time. (Wolpert, *Leading a Life With God*, 68–69.)

From the beginning, Christians have been idealists. Jesus constantly calls us to strive toward the ideal of being perfected "as your heavenly Father is perfect" (Matthew 5:48 [NRSV]). We are to strive toward ideals that we most likely will never achieve, but the striving is what matters. We are to strive joyously, confidently, perseveringly, trusting in grace and not in a neurotic perfectionism that gives way to discouragement or bitterness. The silver may never be without its tarnish, but the polishing makes it shine. (George H. Niederauer, *Precious as Silver: Imagining Your Life With God*, 78.)

Taking Time to Reflect

 Pause and recall what you have read and heard, as well as your own life experiences. Take note of anything that particularly catches your attention—perhaps a word, phrase, or image.

Making Our Requests Known

Focus your prayers more specifically on particular things, persons, or circumstances. The following petitions offer guidance:

Prayers for God's Creation and Our World
Prayers for All God's People
Prayers for the Church and All Who Seek God
Prayers for Our Neighbors
Prayers for Our Families and Friends
Prayers for Ourselves

Thanking God for Our Prayers and Life

What can I give back to the LORD
    for all the good things he has done for me?
I'll lift up the cup of salvation.
    I'll call on the LORD's name.
I'll keep the promises I made to the LORD
    in the presence of all God's people. (Psalm 116:12-14)

Prayer at the End of the Day

Inviting God's Activity

Tender Shepherd of my soul, make yourself and your way known to me in this evening time of prayer and reflection. By the power of your presence, bring me to the end of the day whole, complete, and at peace with you, my neighbor, and myself. Grant a night of peaceful rest and send me forth tomorrow as a witness to your love and grace.

A Continuing Request

Create a clean heart for me, God;
>   put a new, faithful spirit deep inside me! (Psalm 51:10)

Gathering the Day

Remembering—Reflect on the day's experiences.

Confessing—Own up to your own weakness, failure, and sin.

Forgiving—Ask for and accept God's forgiveness, and forgive yourself and all who may have injured you or those you love.

Thanksgiving—Give thanks for the gifts that God has granted this day.

Offering

My whole being clings to you;
>   your strong hand upholds me. (Psalm 63:8)

Blessing

I will lie down and fall asleep in peace
>   because you alone, LORD, let me live in safety. (Psalm 4:8)

Week 44

Where Shall We Sit?

Approaching God with Intention

Have mercy on me, God, according to your faithful love!
> Wipe away my wrongdoings according to your great
> compassion!
Wash me completely clean of my guilt;
> purify me from my sin!
Because I know my wrongdoings,
> my sin is always right in front of me. . . .

Create a clean heart for me, God;
> put a new, faithful spirit deep inside me! (Psalm 51:1-3, 10)

 Sit in silence and stillness for a few moments, lengthening the time each day if you are able.

Becoming Aware of God's Presence

Praise the LORD, all you nations!
> Worship him, all you peoples!
Because God's faithful love toward us is strong,
> the LORD's faithfulness lasts forever!
Praise the LORD! (Psalm 117:1-2)

Inviting God's Intervention

I love the LORD because he hears
    my requests for mercy.
I'll call out to him as long as I live,
    because he listens closely to me. (Psalm 116:1-2)

Listening for God's Voice

Open yourself to hear what God is saying to you through the Scriptures.

Therefore, I have a request for the elders among you. (I ask this as a fellow elder and a witness of Christ's sufferings, and as one who shares in the glory that is about to be revealed.) I urge the elders: Like shepherds, tend the flock of God among you. Watch over it. Don't shepherd because you must, but do it voluntarily for God. Don't shepherd greedily, but do it eagerly. Don't shepherd by ruling over those entrusted to your care, but become examples to the flock. And when the chief shepherd appears, you will receive an unfading crown of glory.

In the same way, I urge you who are younger: accept the authority of the elders. And everyone, clothe yourselves with humility toward each other. God stands against the proud, but he gives favor to the humble. (1 Peter 5:1-5)

Alternative Readings

Matthew 23:1-12
Luke 14:1-14
Psalm 18:27-33
James 4:1-6
Matthew 19:16-22
Luke 16:14-15

Practicing Spiritual Reading

As you read the essay and one or more quotations each day, do so with an openness for further contemplation on the week's theme. Ask God, Is there a word or prayer for my life in these words?

Jesus was invited to a dinner at the home of a religious leader and noticed the rush of many of the guests to get to the head table. He also noticed that those invited all seemed to be well connected, religious leaders, family members, or wealthy neighbors. The Pharisees were watching Jesus to see how he would respond to what they saw as a compromising situation. Once again Jesus rose to the occasion and told a parable about humility and hospitality that must have shocked and shamed the dinner guests (Luke 14:1-14). Jesus was often found in the homes of, and at dinner with, those who were rejected by the religious leaders of his time. . . . He saw each person as a child of God, deeply loved and made worthy by his or her creation by the Creator of all that exists.

The tendency continues even today to separate and classify individuals into categories that are often negative and demeaning. In our honest moments, we confess that we too have bought into this system that says the head table is the place to be. And there are those who watch the followers of Jesus to see how they respond to these artificial categories that separate, denigrate, and elevate persons and divide the human family in unhealthy ways. Will we buy into the system and philosophy that says I want and deserve the best seat in the house? Or, will we really follow Jesus and take the poorest seat because we see everyone as worthy to sit at the head of the table as we are?

Those who forget themselves must, of course, also forget that they are doing so. For once the thought that they are forgetting themselves slips into their consciousness, they are liable to congratulate themselves for it. Self-forgetfulness, it should be noted, is not just disregarding ourselves; it is also focusing attention on something outside us. . . . The self-forgetful person, Kierkegaard tells us, thinks of the sufferings of others, their troubles and pains, and their struggles and losses. She rejoices in their joys and delights in their virtues and accomplishments. She does not insist that people notice her, nor does she insist that she notice herself. Her noticing is centered elsewhere. (Clifford Williams, *Singleness of Heart: Restoring the Divided Soul*, 42-43.)

People are not noble because they succeed or are applauded by others. Their lives are honorable and worthy of emulation because they are striving for what is good—no matter what the results! God asks us to be involved not because we are called to be successful, but because we are called to be *faithful*. Moreover, this very act of faithfulness, no matter how little the impact appears to be, teaches us lessons in perspective and hope which can only be taught by acting compassionately. (Robert J. Wicks, *Everyday Simplicity: A Practical Guide to Spiritual Growth*, 120.)

Remember once again the words of Jesus. Those who make a show of their prayers, their spirituality, have received their reward already. Spirituality at its finest does not call attention to itself. Spirituality at its finest is focused upon and calls attention to God. . . . Spirituality is to walk freely, faithfully, openly, joyfully as liberated children of the living God—at home in God's creation, unafraid of yesterday, today, or tomorrow. One lives, confident that all of life is cared for, nurtured, and preserved by the God of steadfast love without limit. That is cause for celebration and not somberness. (Rueben P. Job, *A Journey Toward Solitude and Community*, 53.)

Taking Time to Reflect

Pause and recall what you have read and heard, as well as your own life experiences. Take note of anything that particularly catches your attention—perhaps a word, phrase, or image.

Making Our Requests Known

Focus your prayers more specifically on particular things, persons, or circumstances. The following petitions offer guidance:

Prayers for God's Creation and Our World
Prayers for All God's People
Prayers for the Church and All Who Seek God
Prayers for Our Neighbors
Prayers for Our Families and Friends
Prayers for Ourselves

Thanking God for Our Prayers and Life

Loving God,
In whom we find our identity
and our life,
thank you for this time with you.
I offer you all of my life
that I am able to give.
Lead me into the light
of your truth and prepare me
for faithful discipleship. Amen.

Prayer at the End of the Day

Inviting God's Activity

Tender Shepherd of my soul, make yourself and your way known to me in this evening time of prayer and reflection. By the power of your presence, bring me to the end of the day whole, complete, and at peace with you, my neighbor, and myself. Grant a night of peaceful rest and send me forth tomorrow as a witness to your love and grace.

A Continuing Request

Create a clean heart for me, God;
    put a new, faithful spirit deep inside me! (Psalm 51:10)

Gathering the Day

Remembering – Reflect on the day's experiences.

Confessing—Own up to your own weakness, failure, and sin.

Forgiving—Ask for and accept God's forgiveness, and forgive yourself and all who may have injured you or those you love.

Thanksgiving—Give thanks for the gifts that God has granted this day.

Offering

My whole being clings to you;
    your strong hand upholds me. (Psalm 63:8)

Blessing

I will lie down and fall asleep in peace
    because you alone, LORD, let me live in safety. (Psalm 4:8)

Week 45

God's Family Includes All God's Children

Approaching God with Intention

Lover of all who are lost,
Uncertain and alone,
Confused and frightened,
Arrogant and disrespectful,
Anxious and fearful,
All who are seeking a safe and secure home,
And all who are already
Comfortably at home in your presence,
Come to me now and
Make yourself known to me
So that I may recognize
And embrace your presence.

 Sit in silence and stillness for a few moments, lengthening the time each day if you are able.

Becoming Aware of God's Presence

I will sing of the Lord's loyal love forever.
   I will proclaim your faithfulness

with my own mouth
from one generation to the next.
That's why I say,
  "Your loyal love is rightly built—forever!
  You establish your faithfulness in heaven." (Psalm 89:1-2)

Inviting God's Intervention

But you, Lord, my Lord!—
  act on my behalf for the sake of your name;
  deliver me because your faithful love is so good;
  because I am poor and needy,
  and my heart is broken. (Psalm 109:21-22)

Listening for God's Voice

Open yourself to hear what God is saying to you through the Scriptures.

Dear friends, let's love each other, because love is from God, and everyone who loves is born from God and knows God. The person who doesn't love does not know God, because God is love. This is how the love of God is revealed to us: God has sent his only Son into the world so that we can live through him. This is love: it is not that we loved God but that he loved us and sent his Son as the sacrifice that deals with our sins.

Dear friends, if God loved us this way, we also ought to love each other. (1 John 4:7-11)

Alternative Readings

Acts 13:44-52
Matthew 15:21-28
Acts 10:9-16
Philemon 1-21
James 2:1-10
Matthew 12:46-50

Practicing Spiritual Reading

As you read the essay and one or more quotations each day, do so with an openness for further contemplation on the week's theme. Ask God, Is there a word or prayer for my life in these words?

There are many who try to squeeze God into a tiny, tiny image of the God made known in Jesus Christ. And most of those efforts are made to determine who is included in God's family. It happened in Jesus' time too. But as the Gospels make clear, Jesus would have none of it and continued to teach and witness to a God whose love was without limits and who embraced every human family as God's own. If the Pharisees could make God small enough, then they could choose who was included in God's family. But Jesus denounced their efforts and often stepped over tradition and rules to demonstrate that no one was left outside the circle of God's love. This is the good news we can receive with joy and proclaim with confidence. Who will you welcome into the Kingdom today?

When we forget who we are and begin to see others as anything less than beloved children of God, we are giving up our identity and our inheritance as children of God. We are no longer following Jesus when we refuse to walk as he walked and refuse to obey his command to love. (Job, *Three Simple Questions*, 46–47.)

The first assumption that I make, therefore, is that God loves me as God loves all people, without qualification. The second is related to it, and it was also a long time coming to me. According to such great early Christian teachers of the first five centuries whom I teach, such as Irenaeus, Athanasius, Anthony, and Gregory of Nyssa, all human beings are created in the image of God. To them, to be in the image of God means that all of us are made for the purpose of knowing and loving God and one another and of being loved in turn, not literally in the same way God knows and loves, but in a way appropriate to human beings. (Bondi, *In Ordinary Time*, 25.)

To follow Jesus is to follow a God made known in Scripture, history, nature, our innermost self, and—most of all—in the life, death, and resurrection of Jesus of Nazareth. To follow Jesus is to follow One who fully trusts in God's goodness, love, and intimate involvement in the affairs of humankind. To follow this Jesus is to desire to be like him in our living and our dying. . . . We do know that following Jesus is the best and only way for us to live fully and faithfully. We really do know that it is the only way to live a peaceful, joyful, fruitful life. . . . (Job, *Three Simple Rules*, 25–26.)

Taking Time to Reflect

Pause and recall what you have read and heard, as well as your own life experiences. Take note of anything that particularly catches your attention—perhaps a word, phrase, or image.

Making Our Requests Known

Focus your prayers more specifically on particular things, persons, or circumstances. The following petitions offer guidance:

Prayers for God's Creation and Our World
Prayers for All God's People
Prayers for the Church and All Who Seek God
Prayers for Our Neighbors
Prayers for Our Families and Friends
Prayers for Ourselves

Thanking God for Our Prayers and Life

God of love and compassion,
author of life and all creation,
I now offer myself to you
so that you might fully
mold and shape me,
as a skilled potter brings forth
something good,
useful, and beautiful
from malleable clay.

Prayer at the End of the Day

Inviting God's Activity

Tender Shepherd of my soul, make yourself and your way known to me in this evening time of prayer and reflection. By the power of your presence, bring me to the end of the day whole, complete, and at peace with you, my neighbor, and myself. Grant a night of peaceful rest and send me forth tomorrow as a witness to your love and grace.

A Continuing Request

Create a clean heart for me, God;
    put a new, faithful spirit deep inside me! (Psalm 51:10)

Gathering the Day

Remembering—Reflect on the day's experiences.

Confessing—Own up to your own weakness, failure, and sin.

Forgiving—Ask for and accept God's forgiveness, and forgive yourself and all who may have injured you or those you love.

Thanksgiving—Give thanks for the gifts that God has granted this day.

Offering

My whole being clings to you;
    your strong hand upholds me. (Psalm 63:8)

Blessing

I will lie down and fall asleep in peace
    because you alone, LORD, let me live in safety. (Psalm 4:8)

Prayer Practice

Releasing Our Fears, Needs, and Hopes

Bringing our fears, needs, and hopes to God in prayer helps us to establish intimacy with God and hear God's voice. Yet releasing our uncertainties to God's care often does not come easily. As we grow to trust God's love and presence, we find this practice to be easier. As a child, I was cradled in my father's lap during a long and serious illness. It was then that I learned that love overcomes fear and offers hope, even in difficult and frightening times. Nearly eighty years later, I know with confidence that the reality of God's love and promise to never forsake us provides these same gifts.

You are encouraged to practice releasing your fears, needs, and hopes into God's care. As you do, invite the Spirit to reassure you of God's love and presence. If anxious thoughts return, take them to God as soon as you are conscious of them and give thanks for God's faithful presence, love, and care. Do this as often as necessary, and you will find that your fears subside as your confidence in God's faithfulness grows.
(Job, *Listen*, 36.)

Week 46

Forgiveness

Approaching God with Intention

Loving God,
May I listen for and hear your faintest whisper,
Feel your slightest touch,
Respond quickly to your call,
Yield to your correction,
Rejoice in your companionship,
And serve you faithfully all the days of my life.

 Sit in silence and stillness for a few moments, lengthening the time each day if you are able.

Becoming Aware of God's Presence

> Praise the LORD!
>   Those who honor the LORD,
>   who adore God's commandments, are truly happy!
> (Psalm 112:1)

Inviting God's Intervention

> Help me, LORD my God!
>   Save me according to your faithful love!
> And let them know that this is by your hand—
>   that you have done it, LORD! (Psalm 109:26-27)

Listening for God's Voice

Open yourself to hear what God is saying to you through the Scriptures.

I thank Christ Jesus our Lord, who has given me strength because he considered me faithful. So he appointed me to ministry even though I used to speak against him, attack his people, and I was proud. But I was shown mercy because I acted in ignorance and without faith. Our Lord's favor poured all over me along with the faithfulness and love that are in Christ Jesus. This saying is reliable and deserves full acceptance: "Christ Jesus came into the world to save sinners"—and I'm the biggest sinner of all. But this is why I was shown mercy, so that Christ Jesus could show his endless patience to me first of all. So I'm an example for those who are going to believe in him for eternal life. Now to the king of the ages, to the immortal, invisible, and only God, may honor and glory be given to him forever and always! Amen. (1 Timothy 1:12-17)

Alternative Readings

Ephesians 4:20-32
Psalm 25:4-11
Matthew 7:1-5
Matthew 26:26-30
1 John 2:12-17
Romans 4:1-8

Practicing Spiritual Reading

As you read the essay and one or more quotations each day, do so with an openness for further contemplation on the week's theme. Ask God, Is there a word or prayer for my life in these words?

Forgiveness is a life-and-death matter because forgiveness lies at the very heart of Christian belief and practice. To remove forgiveness from our theology and practice is to tear the heart out of any hope of faithful Christian discipleship, and it is to drive a stake through the heart of Christian community.

This is the reality we confess every time we pray as Jesus taught us to pray. Forgiveness can never be taken lightly by those who consider their own need of forgiveness. The words of Jesus that we pray bind our need for forgiveness firmly to our willingness to forgive. Forgiveness is not only a preposterous gift; it is unbelievably difficult and costly. That is why we may talk about it easily and practice it with such difficulty. To offer forgiveness to a national enemy today will most likely be branded as unpatriotic and to extend forgiveness to another is often branded as being soft and unrealistic. But the forgiveness Jesus taught and practiced is neither soft nor unpatriotic. But it is extremely costly and laden with a mother lode of grace for those who practice it. To follow Jesus and adopt his values as our own is to love our enemies and desire their good even when they inflict pain and suffering on those we love. The words of Jesus from the cross, "Father forgive them; for they do not know what they are doing," become the final demonstration on how to forgive. His words and action make me realize anew the unparalleled importance of forgiveness and my own timid practice that should be a way of life.

Most mature Christians look back at their lives and see that God has indeed prevented them from painful mistakes, kept them from unworthy goals, and guided them and events around them, even though they were unaware of God's nearness and intervention on their behalf. They also testify that God apprehended them, rather than the other way around. It was God who sought them out, wooed their attention, and called forth their love.

It is this awakening call, this divine spark within, this active involvement in all of life that today is called prevenient grace. (Job, *A Wesleyan Spiritual Reader*, 108.)

The tragedy of our lives is that, while we suffer from the wounds afflicted on us by those who love us, we cannot avoid wounding those we want to love. . . . It is here that we are called to believe deeply in the truth that all fatherhood and all motherhood come from God. Only God is the father and mother who can love us as we need and want to be loved. This belief, when strongly held, can free us not only to forgive our parents, but also to let our children forgive us. (Nouwen, *Here and Now*, 141–142.)

When failure comes, and it is sure to come to all who are in ministry, remember your faithful Savior, Jesus Christ. The redemption offered is adequate for you and me. Do not be reluctant to place your life under the light of Christ for examination. It is a revealing and healing light that brings life and hope. Offer the revealed failures and faults to God with the same abandonment with which you offer yourself. You will discover acceptance and restoration from the hands of the One who made you and loves you. Plan now to establish the way of life and disciplines that can be your counsel and helpers as you seek to walk in fidelity and faithfulness. (Job, *A Guide to Retreat*, 64-65.)

Taking Time to Reflect

 Pause and recall what you have read and heard, as well as your own life experiences. Take note of anything that particularly catches your attention—perhaps a word, phrase, or image.

Making Our Requests Known

Focus your prayers more specifically on particular things, persons, or circumstances. The following petitions offer guidance:

Prayers for God's Creation and Our World
Prayers for All God's People
Prayers for the Church and All Who Seek God
Prayers for Our Neighbors
Prayers for Our Families and Friends
Prayers for Ourselves

Thanking God for Our Prayers and Life

Loving God: make yourself and your way known to me in this time of prayer and reflection. Bring awareness of my faults and confidence in your desire and ability to forgive my sins, heal my wounds, and mend my broken places. By the power of your presence, bring me to be at peace with you, my neighbor, and myself.

Prayer at the End of the Day

Inviting God's Activity

Tender Shepherd of my soul, make yourself and your way known to me in this evening time of prayer and reflection. By the power of your presence, bring me to the end of the day whole, complete, and at peace with you, my neighbor, and myself. Grant a night of peaceful rest and send me forth tomorrow as a witness to your love and grace.

A Continuing Request

Create a clean heart for me, God;
    put a new, faithful spirit deep inside me! (Psalm 51:10)

Gathering the Day

Remembering—Reflect on the day's experiences.

Confessing—Own up to your own weakness, failure, and sin.

Forgiving—Ask for and accept God's forgiveness, and forgive yourself and all who may have injured you or those you love.

Thanksgiving—Give thanks for the gifts that God has granted this day.

Offering

My whole being clings to you;
    your strong hand upholds me. (Psalm 63:8)

Blessing

I will lie down and fall asleep in peace
    because you alone, Lord, let me live in safety. (Psalm 4:8)

Week 47

What Are You Arguing About?

Approaching God with Intention

Creator God
Whose name is love,
Who nurtures and sustains all that is,
Seeks me with clear and tender invitation,
Desiring my constant attentiveness
    so that I may hear every gentle word
    of guidance, assurance, and love,
Speak to me now as I listen
    for your word of truth
For I am yours.

 Sit in silence and stillness for a few moments, lengthening the time each day if you are able.

Becoming Aware of God's Presence

God says, "Because you are devoted to me,
    I'll rescue you.
    I'll protect you because you know my name.
Whenever you cry out to me, I'll answer.
    I'll be with you in troubling times.
    I'll save you and glorify you.

I'll fill you full with old age.
I'll show you my salvation." (Psalm 91:14-16)

Inviting God's Intervention

If the LORD hadn't helped me,
   I would live instantly in total silence.
Whenever I feel my foot slipping,
   your faithful love steadies me, LORD.
When my anxieties multiply,
   your comforting calms me down. (Psalm 94:17-19)

Listening for God's Voice

Open yourself to hear what God is saying to you through the Scriptures.

An argument arose among the disciples about which of them was the greatest. Aware of their deepest thoughts, Jesus took a little child and had the child stand beside him. Jesus said to his disciples, "Whoever welcomes this child in my name welcomes me. Whoever welcomes me, welcomes the one who sent me. Whoever is least among you all is the greatest."

John replied, "Master, we saw someone throwing demons out in your name, and we tried to stop him because he isn't in our group of followers."

But Jesus replied, "Don't stop him, because whoever isn't against you is for you." (Luke 9:46-50)

Alternative Readings

Matthew 23:1-12
Luke 14:7-12
Psalm 145:10-17
1 Corinthians 1:10-17
James 3:13-18
Mark 9:30-37

Practicing Spiritual Reading

As you read the essay and one or more quotations each day, do so with an openness for further contemplation on the week's theme. Ask God, Is there a word or prayer for my life in these words?

As soon as they got in the house at Capernaum, Jesus popped the question that stunned the disciples into complete silence, "What were you arguing about on the way?" No wonder they were speechless; they were arguing about who was the greatest and their silence demonstrated that they knew that what they were arguing about was absolutely contrary to what Jesus had been teaching (Mark 9:33-37).

Sometimes I wonder if the arguing in the church would turn to deafening silence if we listened to and heard the voice of Jesus saying to us, "What are you arguing about?" Who is in and who is out, who is great and who is small, who is worthy and who is not, who is loved and who is not—all are questions Jesus settled long ago and yet they are so often the center of our conversations.

When this happened with the Twelve, Jesus sat down and called them to him and explained once more what it meant to live in the kingdom of God. He explained once again what it meant to follow him and to be like him. Rather than arguing, perhaps we should be asking Jesus to make his way plain to us this day and every day.

 The creed's most radical and important confession comes right at the beginning: "We believe in one God." It is the root out of which all the rest grows. Without it nothing more can be said. . . . All language about God reaches into a mystery it cannot grasp or comprehend. Yet we need all the language we can get, since we recognize that, in the end, all language falls short. (Johnson, *The Creed*, 65–66)

The central theme in [Jesus'] personal life was the growing intimacy with, trust in, and love of his Abba. He lived securely in his Father's acceptance. "As the Father has loved me so have I loved you" (John 15:9 [The Jerusalem Bible]), he reassures us. Jesus' inner life was centered in God. His communion with his Abba transformed his vision of reality, enabling him to perceive divine love toward sinners and scalawags. Jesus did not live from himself or for himself but from the graciousness of the Other, who is incomprehensibly caring. He understood his Father's compassionate heart. (Manning, *Ruthless Trust*, 125.)

Dorothy Day is said to have seen Christ in everyone. She found Christ in bowery derelicts, in Nazis, in Communists, and in cardinals who admired Senator Joseph McCarthy. She loved everyone who detested everyone else. She refused to fit anyone's philosophy or political mold and thereby discovered spirituality in the secular and the divine in the mundane. Yes, for the political mystic God is a shout in the streets—the shouts of joy and sorrow, the shouts of hope and of pain, the shouts of our neighbor and of the stranger, the shouts of the mighty and the meek—the shouts of the loud and "the least of these my brethren." (Donald E. Messer, *Contemporary Images of Christian Ministry,* 129.)

Taking Time to Reflect

Pause and recall what you have read and heard, as well as your own life experiences. Take note of anything that particularly catches your attention—perhaps a word, phrase, or image.

Making Our Requests Known

Focus your prayers more specifically on particular things, persons, or circumstances. The following petitions offer guidance:

Prayers for God's Creation and Our World
Prayers for All God's People
Prayers for the Church and All Who Seek God
Prayers for Our Neighbors
Prayers for Our Families and Friends
Prayers for Ourselves

Thanking God for Our Prayers and Life

Establish justice for me, God!
    Argue my case against ungodly people!
    Rescue me from the dishonest and unjust!
Because you are my God, my protective fortress!
    Why have you rejected me?
    Why do I have to walk around,
        sad, oppressed by enemies?
Send your light and truth—those will guide me!
    Let them bring me to your holy mountain,
        to your dwelling place.
Let me come to God's altar—
let me come to God, my joy, my delight—
    then I will give you thanks with the lyre,
    God, my God! (Psalm 43:1-4)

Prayer at the End of the Day

Inviting God's Activity

Tender Shepherd of my soul, make yourself and your way known to me in this evening time of prayer and reflection. By the power of your presence, bring me to the end of the day whole, complete, and at peace with you, my neighbor, and myself. Grant a night of peaceful rest and send me forth tomorrow as a witness to your love and grace.

A Continuing Request

Create a clean heart for me, God;
    put a new, faithful spirit deep inside me! (Psalm 51:10)

Gathering the Day

Remembering—Reflect on the day's experiences.

Confessing—Own up to your own weakness, failure, and sin.

Forgiving—Ask for and accept God's forgiveness, and forgive yourself and all who may have injured you or those you love.

Thanksgiving—Give thanks for the gifts that God has granted this day.

Offering

My whole being clings to you;
    your strong hand upholds me. (Psalm 63:8)

Blessing

I will lie down and fall asleep in peace
    because you alone, Lord, let me live in safety. (Psalm 4:8)

Week 48

God Is at Work in You

Approaching God with Intention

God of love, holiness, and strength, we thank you for the gift of your presence through the morning hours. Continue to make yourself and your way known to us throughout the remaining hours of the day. Grant us grace to follow you in faithfulness, joy, and peace. We are yours.

 Sit in silence and stillness for a few moments, lengthening the time each day if you are able.

Becoming Aware of God's Presence

Praise the LORD!
Praise the LORD from heaven!
    Praise God on the heights!
Praise God, all of you who are his messengers!
    Praise God, all of you who comprise his heavenly forces!
                                            (Psalm 148:1-2)

Inviting God's Intervention

Stretch out your hand from above!
    Rescue me and deliver me from deep water. . . .
                                            (Psalm 144:7a)

Listening for God's Voice

Open yourself to hear what God is saying to you through the Scriptures.

Therefore, my loved ones, just as you always obey me, not just when I am present but now even more while I am away, carry out your own salvation with fear and trembling. God is the one who enables you both to want and to actually live out his good purposes. Do everything without grumbling and arguing so that you may be blameless and pure, innocent children of God surrounded by people who are crooked and corrupt. Among these people you shine like stars in the world because you hold on to the word of life. This will allow me to say on the day of Christ that I haven't run for nothing or worked for nothing. But even if I am poured out like a drink offering upon the altar of service for your faith, I am glad. I'm glad with all of you. You should be glad about this in the same way. Be glad with me!
(Philippians 2:12-18)

Alternative Readings

Matthew 10:40-42
James 1:2-8
James 1:12-18
2 Corinthians 3:12-18
1 Corinthians 3:16-23
Luke 12:4-12

Practicing Spiritual Reading

As you read the essay and one or more quotations each day, do so with an openness for further contemplation on the week's theme. Ask God, Is there a word or prayer for my life in these words?

God at work in you is an explosive, earthshaking, and life-changing truth. It is a truth expressed throughout the biblical witness and so very clearly in Philippians 2:13. At this very moment, whoever and wherever you are, something beyond our full comprehension is taking place within your life and mine. The infinite God of love has chosen to become resident within you and to work within you for pure good. Since God is pure goodness and has no ulterior motives, we can trust, embrace, and cooperate with the divine work going on within us and every child of God.

Once we accept this truth and fully embrace this Divine Presence within us, many other things become clear and possible. We can listen to and follow the guidance of the One who made us, loves us, and is able to lead us in the way of God. We can hear and respond to the Divine call to communion and community with the present and living God. We can hear and respond to the call to faithfulness and service because we are no longer on our own, but the power and the presence of the God at work within us is ready, available, and capable to form, transform, and shape us into the beautiful, faithful, and good persons we were created to become. We can now walk through each day without fear because we remember that we do not walk alone but always with the companionship and help of the One who is now at work within us. Let's remember and remind each other often of this radical and revolutionary truth.

 The care of the soul is a lifelong practice that is often relegated to second or even last place in our lives. We are so immersed in the demands of our noisy world that we can easily ignore the chronic emptiness deep within. The emptiness ranges from a dull ache on the edge of our awareness to a sharp pain calling all of our attention to itself. As Pascal has said, "Only God can fill a God-shaped emptiness," And only God can remove the ache of our soul. (Job, *A Guide to Retreat*, 12.)

To adore is to open wide our souls to God who is already there. That is also the beginning of communion. There is communion between God and the individual soul, communion with the Body of Christ as the Communion of Saints, and communion with Christ through the sharing of His Spirit. (Grace Adolphsen Brame, introduction to Underhill, *The Ways of the Spirit*, 30–31.)

Living a forgiven life is more than simply relief that we have been absolved. Forgiveness is living with the abiding sense of what our relationship with God and other people can be, and so forgiveness motivates us, admonishes us, provokes us to enrich our poor relationships. Or as Abraham Lincoln put it to a startled questioner near the end of the Civil War: "Madam, do I not destroy my enemies when I make them my friends?" God has destroyed us as enemies, and made us friends, which pivots us outward to destroy our own enemies by making them our friends. Prayer is friendship. (James C. Howell, *The Beautiful Work of Learning to Pray: 31 Lessons*, 74.)

In religious circles we find today a fierce and almost violent planning and programming, a sense that without ceaseless activity nothing will ever be accomplished. How seldom it occurs to us that God has to undo and do all over again so much of what we in our willfulness have pushed through in [God's] name. How little there is in us of the silent and radiant strength in which the secret works of God really take place! How ready we are to speak, how loathe to listen, to sense the further dimension of what it is that we confront. (Steere, *Dimensions of Prayer*, 4–5.)

Taking Time to Reflect

Pause and recall what you have read and heard, as well as your own life experiences. Take note of anything that particularly catches your attention—perhaps a word, phrase, or image.

Making Our Requests Known

Focus your prayers more specifically on particular things, persons, or circumstances. The following petitions offer guidance:

Prayers for God's Creation and Our World
Prayers for All God's People
Prayers for the Church and All Who Seek God
Prayers for Our Neighbors
Prayers for Our Families and Friends
Prayers for Ourselves

Thanking God for Our Prayers and Life

May the God of peace and love
dwell within us, accompany us,
guide us, and keep us
throughout the day and always. Amen.

Prayer at the End of the Day

Inviting God's Activity

Tender Shepherd of my soul, make yourself and your way known to me in this evening time of prayer and reflection. By the power of your presence, bring me to the end of the day whole, complete, and at peace with you, my neighbor, and myself. Grant a night of peaceful rest and send me forth tomorrow as a witness to your love and grace.

A Continuing Request

Create a clean heart for me, God;
> put a new, faithful spirit deep inside me! (Psalm 51:10)

Gathering the Day

Remembering—Reflect on the day's experiences.

Confessing—Own up to your own weakness, failure, and sin.

Forgiving—Ask for and accept God's forgiveness, and forgive yourself and all who may have injured you or those you love.

Thanksgiving—Give thanks for the gifts that God has granted this day.

Offering

My whole being clings to you;
> your strong hand upholds me. (Psalm 63:8)

Blessing

I will lie down and fall asleep in peace
> because you alone, LORD, let me live in safety. (Psalm 4:8)

Week 49

Living as a Child of God

Approaching God with Intention

Loving God,
Remind me often today where I find my identity.
May I never forget that I am your beloved child.
May I listen for and hear your faintest whisper,
Feel your slightest touch,
Respond quickly to your call,
Yield to your word of correction,
Rejoice in your companionship,
And serve you faithfully all the days of my life. Amen.

 Sit in silence and stillness for a few moments, lengthening the time each day if you are able.

Becoming Aware of God's Presence

> Listen to me, you who look for righteousness, you who seek the
> LORD:
> Look to the rock from which you were cut
>   and to the quarry where you were dug. . . .
>
> Pay attention to me, my people;
>   listen to me, my nation,

for teaching will go out from me,
  my justice, as a light to the nations. (Isaiah 51:1, 4)

Inviting God's Intervention

But now, LORD, you are our father.
  We are the clay, and you are our potter.
  All of us are the work of your hand. (Isaiah 64:8)

Listening for God's Voice

Open yourself to hear what God is saying to you through the Scriptures.

The light was in the world,
  and the world came into being through the light,
    but the world didn't recognize the light.
The light came to his own people,
  and his own people didn't welcome him.
But those who did welcome him,
    those who believed in his name,
  he authorized to become God's children,
    born not from blood
    nor from human desire or passion,
    but born from God.
The Word became flesh
  and made his home among us.
We have seen his glory,
  glory like that of a father's only son,
    full of grace and truth. (John 1:10-14)

Alternative Readings
1 John 3:1-6
Matthew 18:1-5
Matthew 19:13-15
Isaiah 40:6-11
Ephesians 4:7-16
Romans 8:12-17

Practicing Spiritual Reading

As you read the essay and one or more quotations each day, do so with an openness for further contemplation on the week's theme. Ask God, Is there a word or prayer for my life in these words?

They just didn't get it. Time and time again Jesus demonstrated to the disciples what it means to live as a faithful child of God. And time and time again the ways of the culture and their old habits got the best of them and they found themselves vying for the best seats, the places of power, the recognition of their rank among the Twelve, and the willingness to manipulate the system to get what they wanted.

My temptation is to be harsh and judgmental toward the Twelve. But then, I stop to think about the world in which they lived and realize that for the most part they had taken a giant leap of faith out of and over the culture of their time to a more faithful way of living. Yes, they stumbled now and then. But for the most part, they kept their eye on and tried to practice what Jesus taught and lived in their presence every day. That is what I am going to try today and every day that God grants to me. It will take a giant leap of faith to get out of and over the expectations and practices of the culture in which we live, but the way of living that Jesus offers is a million to one winner over what our culture offers. Let's help each other practice what Jesus taught and lived.

 The doubt with which we need to temper certainty is a searching doubt. It consists of a perpetual attitude of self-scrutiny, of not being content with the way we are, of poking around behind appearances, and of interrogating ourselves. . . .To be sure, this doubt can . . . cause us to turn inward too much and make us think that we will never know what our status with God is. . . . In spite of these risks, doubt is necessary, for without it we are not likely to move toward singleness of heart. Though it may seem paradoxical, a childlike faith requires the very thing which, if indulged in, would undermine it. (Williams, *Singleness of Heart*, 139.)

There are many practices that establish who we are and remind us who we are as God's beloved children. Whenever we share God's grace, mercy, compassion, forgiveness, and love, we act as children of God. And in doing so, we confirm our identity as children of God. Our identity is not something we create but something that is given by the God who made us, leads us, sustains us, and loves us. We discover more of the full meaning of our identity as we seek a growing relationship with God through our acts of prayer and worship. (Job, *Three Simple Questions*, 45.)

Everything that came from Jesus' lips worked like a magnifying glass to focus human awareness on the two most important facts about life: God's overwhelming love of humanity, and the need for people to accept that love and let it flow through them in the way water passes without obstruction through a sea anemone. (Smith, *The Soul of Christianity*, 53–54.)

Taking Time to Reflect

Pause and recall what you have read and heard, as well as your own life experiences. Take note of anything that particularly catches your attention—perhaps a word, phrase, or image.

Making Our Requests Known

Focus your prayers more specifically on particular things, persons, or circumstances. The following petitions offer guidance:

Prayers for God's Creation and Our World
Prayers for All God's People
Prayers for the Church and All Who Seek God
Prayers for Our Neighbors
Prayers for Our Families and Friends
Prayers for Ourselves

Thanking God for Our Prayers and Life

I pray that the LORD answers you
    whenever you are in trouble.
  Let the name of Jacob's God protect you.
Let God send help to you from the sanctuary
  and support you from Zion.
Let God recall your many grain offerings;
  let him savor your entirely burned offerings. *Selah*
Let God grant what is in your heart
  and fulfill all your plans.
Then we will rejoice that you've been helped.
  We will fly our flags in the name of our God.
  Let the LORD fulfill all your requests! (Psalm 20:1-5)

Prayer at the End of the Day

Inviting God's Activity

Tender Shepherd of my soul, make yourself and your way known to me in this evening time of prayer and reflection. By the power of your presence, bring me to the end of the day whole, complete, and at peace with you, my neighbor, and myself. Grant a night of peaceful rest and send me forth tomorrow as a witness to your love and grace.

A Continuing Request

Create a clean heart for me, God;
    put a new, faithful spirit deep inside me! (Psalm 51:10)

Gathering the Day

Remembering—Reflect on the day's experiences.

Confessing—Own up to your own weakness, failure, and sin.

Forgiving—Ask for and accept God's forgiveness, and forgive yourself and all who may have injured you or those you love.

Thanksgiving—Give thanks for the gifts that God has granted this day.

Offering

My whole being clings to you;
    your strong hand upholds me. (Psalm 63:8)

Blessing

I will lie down and fall asleep in peace
    because you alone, LORD, let me live in safety. (Psalm 4:8)

Privilege and Responsibility of Riches

Approaching God with Intention

Loving God,
I bring myself into your presence
Not to tell you what to do
But to invite you to be my honored guest
As I offer you all that I am
All that I hope to become
And invite your transforming presence
To shape me more and more into your
Beloved and faithful child.
Amen.

 Sit in silence and stillness for a few moments, lengthening the time each day if you are able.

Becoming Aware of God's Presence

Who could possibly compare to the LORD our God?
> God rules from on high;
>> he has to come down to even see heaven and earth!
God lifts up the poor from the dirt

and raises up the needy from the garbage pile
    to seat them with leaders—
with the leaders of his own people! (Psalm 113:5-8)

Inviting God's Intervention

So I called on the LORD's name:
    "LORD, please save me!"
The LORD is merciful and righteous;
    our God is compassionate. (Psalm 116:4-5)

Listening for God's Voice

Open yourself to hear what God is saying to you through the Scriptures.

The believers devoted themselves to the apostles' teaching, to the community, to their shared meals, and to their prayers. A sense of awe came over everyone. God performed many wonders and signs through the apostles. All the believers were united and shared everything. They would sell pieces of property and possessions and distribute the proceeds to everyone who needed them. Every day, they met together in the temple and ate in their homes. They shared food with gladness and simplicity. They praised God and demonstrated God's goodness to everyone. The Lord added daily to the community those who were being saved.
(Acts 2:42-47)

Alternative Readings

Luke 18:18-30
Exodus 32:1-8
2 Thessalonians 3:6-16
Mark 12:41-44
2 Peter 3:14-18
Matthew 6:19-21

Practicing Spiritual Reading

As you read the essay and one or more quotations each day, do so with an openness for further contemplation on the week's theme. Ask God, Is there a word or prayer for my life in these words?

The awareness of failure can nibble away at our peaceful heart and even our effectiveness as disciples. But there is a remedy. There is a "cure for the sinsick soul." It is well to keep this truth in mind when we discuss those times when covenant is shattered by some obvious and horrendous act of infidelity and disobedience. Is there still remedy? The answer is obvious. Of course! Complete cure is guaranteed. It is Jesus who heals the sick, gives sight to the blind, raises the dead, and forgives the sinner.

There is no question of cure. But there first must be an examination, confession, and repentance. Richard Foster speaks of the "Prayer of Examen." It is a time when we invite God to scrutinize every facet of our existence. We not only invite the Lord to scrutinize our deepest self, but we ask that the light, the healing light, the purifying light, the life-giving light of Christ's presence touch our failure and our most broken self. Yes, there is remedy for our woundedness. Complete cure is assured. . . .

That cure is offered in Christ through whom "we have redemption . . . according to the riches of his grace" (Ephesians 1:7 NRSV). (Job, *A Guide to Retreat*, 63.)

The mystery of God's grace is deeper than we think. It washes away all lesser attainments. Of all God's creatures, only we are cursed with the consciousness of an unreturning past, and only we are privileged to contemplate the end and purpose of life—not just our own lives or our work, but the end and purpose of life itself. Our perishable accomplishments find their meaning only as we derive it from the eternal presence and imperishable purposes of God. We are saved by grace. (Robert Schnase, *Ambition in Ministry: Our Spiritual Struggle with Success, Achievement, and Competition*, 124–125.)

"The love of money," we know, "is the root of all evil;" but not the thing itself. The fault does not lie in the money, but in them that use it. It may be used ill: And what may not? But it may likewise be used well: . . . it is an excellent gift of God, answering the noblest ends. In the hands of his children, it is food for the hungry, drink for the thirsty, raiment for the naked: It gives to the traveller and the stranger where to lay his head. . . . We may be a defence for the oppressed, a means of health to the sick, of ease to them that are in pain; it may be as eyes to the blind, as feet to the lame; yea, a lifter up from the gates of death! (Wesley, "Sermon 50, The Use of Money," *Works*, 2:263.)

Nearly every time he speaks for any length of time, mostly to tell stories or to suggest to the disciples they've missed the point once again, Jesus finds a way to work in some thoughts on living abundantly. . . . Only he'd never have made the best-seller list, given that his road to riches and security always begins with emptying out—of possessions, of self. . . . (Jordan-Lake, *Why Jesus Makes Me Nervous*, 25–26.)

Taking Time to Reflect

Pause and recall what you have read and heard, as well as your own life experiences. Take note of anything that particularly catches your attention—perhaps a word, phrase, or image.

Making Our Requests Known

Focus your prayers more specifically on particular things, persons, or circumstances. The following petitions offer guidance:

Prayers for God's Creation and Our World
Prayers for All God's People
Prayers for the Church and All Who Seek God
Prayers for Our Neighbors
Prayers for Our Families and Friends
Prayers for Ourselves

Thanking God for Our Prayers and Life

Here am I,
my loving Creator.

Accept the gift I bring
and make it fruitful
as you keep me faithful,
for I am yours.

Prayer at the End of the Day

Inviting God's Activity

Tender Shepherd of my soul, make yourself and your way known to me in this evening time of prayer and reflection. By the power of your presence, bring me to the end of the day whole, complete, and at peace with you, my neighbor, and myself. Grant a night of peaceful rest and send me forth tomorrow as a witness to your love and grace.

A Continuing Request

Create a clean heart for me, God;
    put a new, faithful spirit deep inside me! (Psalm 51:10)

Gathering the Day

Remembering—Reflect on the day's experiences.

Confessing—Own up to your own weakness, failure, and sin.

Forgiving—Ask for and accept God's forgiveness, and forgive yourself and all who may have injured you or those you love.

Thanksgiving—Give thanks for the gifts that God has granted this day.

Offering

My whole being clings to you;
    your strong hand upholds me. (Psalm 63:8)

Blessing

I will lie down and fall asleep in peace
    because you alone, LORD, let me live in safety. (Psalm 4:8)

Week 51

To Whom Do We Belong?

Approaching God with Intention

God of love, holiness, and strength, I thank you for the gift of your presence. Continue to make yourself and your way known to me throughout this day. Grant me grace to follow you in faithfulness, joy, and peace. I am yours.

 Sit in silence and stillness for a few moments, lengthening the time each day if you are able.

Becoming Aware of God's Presence

Seek the LORD when he can still be found;
 call him while he is yet near.
Let the wicked abandon their ways
 and the sinful their schemes.
Let them return to the LORD so that he may have mercy on them,
 to our God, because he is generous with forgiveness.

             (Isaiah 55:6-7)

Inviting God's Intervention

Examine me, God! Look at my heart!
 Put me to the test! Know my anxious thoughts!
Look to see if there is any idolatrous way in me,
 then lead me on the eternal path! (Psalm 139:23-24)

Listening for God's Voice

Open yourself to hear what God is saying to you through the Scriptures.

Then the Pharisees met together to find a way to trap Jesus in his words. They sent their disciples, along with the supporters of Herod, to him. "Teacher," they said, "we know that you are genuine and that you teach God's way as it really is. We know that you are not swayed by people's opinions, because you don't show favoritism. So tell us what you think: Does the Law allow people to pay taxes to Caesar or not?"

Knowing their evil motives, Jesus replied, "Why do you test me, you hypocrites? Show me the coin used to pay the tax." And they brought him a denarion. "Whose image and inscription is this?" he asked.

"Caesar's," they replied.

Then he said, "Give to Caesar what belongs to Caesar and to God what belongs to God." When they heard this they were astonished, and they departed. (Matthew 22:15-22)

Alternative Readings

Romans 15:14-21
Galatians 6:1-10
Luke 20:20-26
Luke 23:1-5
1 Corinthians 3:1-9
John 10:11-18

Practicing Spiritual Reading

As you read the essay and one or more quotations each day, do so with an openness for further contemplation on the week's theme. Ask God, Is there a word or prayer for my life in these words?

They were out to trap Jesus. It still happens today that leaders, religious and other kinds as well, are asked questions to trap them into saying something that will discredit them or make the questioner look superior. Well, it didn't work with Jesus. The question was about paying taxes (Matthew 22:15-22), and Jesus immediately saw through their scheme and said, "Show me the coin used to pay the tax." When they produced the coin Jesus asked, "Whose image and inscription is this?" They answered, "Caesar's." Jesus then said, "Give to Caesar what belongs to Caesar and to God what belongs to God."

It is wonderful to belong, and there are countless lesser gods hidden in the glitter of our culture with subtle and flagrant invitations seeking our loyalty and allegiance. However, from the very beginning Christians have maintained that we have been made in the image of God and therefore belong ultimately and only to God in Christ. Often this has been a costly choice, sometimes even demanding the life of the one who maintained loyalty to God in Christ above all else. But the decision was always and ultimately right and rewarding. The Heidelberg Catechism declares that "We belong—body and soul, in life and in death—not to ourselves, but to our faithful Savior, Jesus Christ." It is the biblical witness of who God is and who we are and to whom we belong. And it is enough to keep us safe, secure, and faithful in this troubled world and bring us safely home to our eternal dwelling. It is hard to think of belonging to anyone else.

Experiencing God's love means experiencing that one has been unreservedly accepted, approved, and infinitely loved, that one can and should accept oneself and one's neighbour. Salvation is joy in God which expresses itself in joy in and with one's neighbour. (Walter Kasper, *Jesus the Christ*, 86.)

Before any pragmatic, utilitarian, or altruistic motivations, prayer is born of a desire to be with Jesus. . . . To really love someone implies a natural longing for presence and intimate communion. . . . Trappist monk Basil Pennington . . . writes, "A father is delighted when his little one, leaving off his toys and friends, runs to him and climbs into his arms. . . . Our Centering Prayer is much like that. We settle down in our Father's arms, in his loving hands. Our mind, our thoughts, our imaginations may flit about here and there . . . but essentially we are choosing to remain for this time intimately with our Father, giving ourselves to him, receiving his love and care, letting him enjoy us as he will. (Manning, *A Glimpse of Jesus*, 83–85.)

For those who live at home with God in this world, the concept of a home prepared for us when we transition from this life to the next is no longer threatening but deeply affirming. The promise of Jesus, "When I go to prepare a place for you, I will return and take you to be with me so that where I am you will be too," gives us confidence to live fully and unafraid in every circumstance of life (John 14:3). (Job, *Life Stories*, 89.)

Taking Time to Reflect

Pause and recall what you have read and heard, as well as your own life experiences. Take note of anything that particularly catches your attention—perhaps a word, phrase, or image.

Making Our Requests Known

Focus your prayers more specifically on particular things, persons, or circumstances. The following petitions offer guidance:

Prayers for God's Creation and Our World
Prayers for All God's People
Prayers for the Church and All Who Seek God
Prayers for Our Neighbors
Prayers for Our Families and Friends
Prayers for Ourselves

Thanking God for Our Prayers and Life

But now, says the LORD—
the one who created you, Jacob,
    the one who formed you, Israel:
Don't fear, for I have redeemed you;
    I have called you by name; you are mine.
When you pass through the waters, I will be with you;
    when through the rivers, they won't sweep over you.
When you walk through the fire, you won't be scorched
    and flame won't burn you.
I am the LORD your God,
    the holy one of Israel, your savior.
I have given Egypt as your ransom,
    Cush and Seba in your place.
Because you are precious in my eyes,
    you are honored, and I love you. (Isaiah 43:1-4a)

Prayer at the End of the Day

Inviting God's Activity

Tender Shepherd of my soul, make yourself and your way known to me in this evening time of prayer and reflection. By the power of your presence, bring me to the end of the day whole, complete, and at peace with you, my neighbor, and myself. Grant a night of peaceful rest and send me forth tomorrow as a witness to your love and grace.

A Continuing Request

Create a clean heart for me, God;
> put a new, faithful spirit deep inside me! (Psalm 51:10)

Gathering the Day

Remembering—Reflect on the day's experiences.

Confessing—Own up to your own weakness, failure, and sin.

Forgiving—Ask for and accept God's forgiveness, and forgive yourself and all who may have injured you or those you love.

Thanksgiving—Give thanks for the gifts that God has granted this day.

Offering

My whole being clings to you;
> your strong hand upholds me. (Psalm 63:8)

Blessing

I will lie down and fall asleep in peace
> because you alone, LORD, let me live in safety. (Psalm 4:8)

Week 52

All Things Are Possible With God

Approaching God with Intention

Loving God, lead me to find a healthy balance
  between being and doing.
Set me free from the bondage of unrealistic expectations
  and fill me with your enabling presence this very day.
I offer my prayer in the name of Jesus Christ
  whose life was a perfect balance of doing and being. Amen.

Practicing Stillness

 Sit in silence and stillness for a few moments, lengthening the time each day if you are able.

Becoming Aware of God's Presence

All you who serve the Lord: bless the Lord right now!
  All you who minister in the Lord's house at night: bless God!
Lift up your hands to the sanctuary
  and bless the Lord! (Psalm 134:1-2)

Inviting God's Intervention

> Lᴏʀᴅ, do good to people who are good,
> to people whose hearts are right. (Psalm 125:4)

Listening for God's Voice

Open yourself to hear what God is saying to you through the Scriptures.

As Jesus moved forward, he faced smothering crowds. A woman was there who had been bleeding for twelve years. She had spent her entire livelihood on doctors, but no one could heal her. She came up behind him and touched the hem of his clothes, and at once her bleeding stopped.

"Who touched me?" Jesus asked.

When everyone denied it, Peter said, "Master, the crowds are surrounding you and pressing in on you!"

But Jesus said, "Someone touched me. I know that power has gone out from me."

When the woman saw that she couldn't escape notice, she came trembling and fell before Jesus. In front of everyone, she explained why she had touched him and how she had been immediately healed.

"Daughter, your faith has healed you," Jesus said. "Go in peace." (Luke 8:42-48)

Alternative Readings
Luke 19:1-10
2 Corinthians 7:2-12
1 Samuel 12:1-5
1 Timothy 1:12-17
Ezekiel 34:11-16
Mark 2:13-17

Practicing Spiritual Reading

As you read the essay and one or more quotations each day, do so with an openness for further contemplation on the week's theme. Ask God, Is there a word or prayer for my life in these words?

It is such a mess that it seems hopeless! We say that about our world, our current global economic situation, the life of a wounded and lost soul, and sometimes even we say it deep in the quiet places of our hearts about ourselves. But when we do we miss the point of much of what Jesus taught. The story of Zacchaeus in Luke 19 is an illustration of God doing the impossible. First of all, Jesus breaks all the cultural and religious barriers by treating a hated tax collector with respect and dignity and then invites himself to dinner at the tax collector's home. A shocking transformation of cultural and religious patterns that seemed unchangeable. And then Jesus heard Zacchaeus declare he would give half his accumulated wealth to the poor. And further, that if there were any fraudulent activity he would repay the amount taken four times over. Here we have a perfect example of God doing what is impossible for mere mortals alone as this rich tax collector, lost and alienated, is "saved" and welcomed home to the kingdom of God (Luke 19:9-10; compare Matthew 19:23-26). What is on your horizon this week that seems impossible to mere mortals? Why not let it be the focus of your prayers as you ask God to intervene? Perhaps we could all take a lesson from the persistence of the widow who would not relent in her fervent quest for justice until her request was fulfilled (Luke 18:1-8).

 Before anything else, above all else, beyond everything else, God loves us. God loves us extravagantly, ridiculously, without limit or condition. God is in love with us; God is besotted with us. God yearns for us. . . . God loves us hopelessly as mothers love their babies. . . . God loves us, the very people we are; and not only that, but, even against what we ourselves find plausible, God *likes* us. (Bondi, *In Ordinary Time*, 22–23.)

I remember the first day I came home. There were four beautiful women walking out onto the porch to say hello. I looked at the gated yard and had a strange feeling that it seemed familiar. I realized that I had lost my way long ago, and coming into this place gave me an almost forgotten sense of peace. When I walked in, there were plants everywhere; and I was crying because of the nice furniture. I loved the soft bed that felt completely different than the prison mattress I had just left. When I went into the kitchen, I rejoiced at the pots and pans, because I remembered the glass jars and spoons I had left on the sidewalk. This was the home I'd almost forgotten about. Thank you, God, for leading me home. (The Women of Magdalene, *Find Your Way Home*, 104.)

Every now and then we see splendid examples of what it means to follow God as made known in Jesus. These persons, both young and old, live out the gospel in such clear ways that their lives can be explained only by God's dwelling within them. "How like Jesus! How like God!" we may exclaim as we observe their lives of compassion, love, and grace. As we see them living as Jesus taught us to live, in our hearts we whisper, "I want to be like that; I want to live like that; I want to belong to God like that." And we can love like that; we can live like that. (Job, *Three Simple Questions*, 30.)

Taking Time to Reflect

Pause and recall what you have read and heard, as well as your own life experiences. Take note of anything that particularly catches your attention—perhaps a word, phrase, or image.

Making Our Requests Known

Focus your prayers more specifically on particular things, persons, or circumstances. The following petitions offer guidance:

Prayers for God's Creation and Our World
Prayers for All God's People
Prayers for the Church and All Who Seek God
Prayers for Our Neighbors
Prayers for Our Families and Friends
Prayers for Ourselves

Thanking God for Our Prayers and Life

Don't you know? Haven't you heard?
    The LORD is the everlasting God,
    the creator of the ends of the earth.
    He doesn't grow tired or weary.
His understanding is beyond human reach,
    giving power to the tired
    and reviving the exhausted.
Youths will become tired and weary,
    young men will certainly stumble;
    but those who hope in the LORD
    will renew their strength;
    they will fly up on wings like eagles;
    they will run and not be tired;
    they will walk and not be weary. (Isaiah 40:28-31)

Prayer at the End of the Day

Inviting God's Activity

Tender Shepherd of my soul, make yourself and your way known to me in this evening time of prayer and reflection. By the power of your presence, bring me to the end of the day whole, complete, and at peace with you, my neighbor, and myself. Grant a night of peaceful rest and send me forth tomorrow as a witness to your love and grace.

A Continuing Request

Create a clean heart for me, God;
> put a new, faithful spirit deep inside me! (Psalm 51:10)

Gathering the Day

Remembering—Reflect on the day's experiences.

Confessing—Own up to your own weakness, failure, and sin.

Forgiving—Ask for and accept God's forgiveness, and forgive yourself and all who may have injured you or those you love.

Thanksgiving—Give thanks for the gifts that God has granted this day.

Offering

My whole being clings to you;
> your strong hand upholds me. (Psalm 63:8)

Blessing

I will lie down and fall asleep in peace
> because you alone, LORD, let me live in safety. (Psalm 4:8)

Bibliography

Barron, Robert. *The Strangest Way: Walking the Christian Path*.
Maryknoll, NY: Orbis, 2002.

Bass, Dorothy C., and Craig Dykstra. "Practicing a Way of Life." 193–202.
Practicing Our Faith: A Way of Life for a Searching People. Edited by
Dorothy C. Bass. San Francisco. Jossey-Bass, 1997.

Blumhardt, Christoph Friedrich. "Action in Waiting." 1–13. *Watch for
the Light: Readings for Advent and Christmas*. Walden, NY: Plough
Publishing, 2001.

Bondi, Roberta C. *In Ordinary Time: Healing the Wounds of the Heart*.
Nashville: Abingdon, 1996.

Brame, Grace Adolphsen. Introduction to *The Ways of the Spirit* by
Evelyn Underhill. New York: Crossroad, 1993.

———. *Faith, the Yes of the Heart*. Minneapolis: Augsburg Fortress, 1999.

Brueggemann, Walter, "Covenantal Spirituality," in *New Conversations*
(The United Church of Christ, out of print), 8.

Bruteau, Beatrice. *Radical Optimism: Rooting Ourselves in Reality*. New
York: Crossroad, 1993.

Casey, Michael. *Toward God: The Ancient Wisdom of Western Prayer*.
Liguori, MO: Liguori/Triumph, 1996.

Chittister, Joan. *Illuminated Life: Monastic Wisdom for Seekers of Light*.
Maryknoll, NY: Orbis, 2000.

Dykstra, Craig, and Dorothy C. Bass. "Times of Yearning, Practices of Faith." 1–12. *Practicing Our Faith: A Way of Life for a Searching People.* Edited by Dorothy C. Bass. San Francisco. Jossey-Bass, 1997.

Fénelon, François. *The Royal Way of the Cross.* Edited by Hal M. Helms. Brewster, MA: Paraclete, 1982.

Foster, Richard J. *Prayer: Finding the Heart's True Home.* New York: HarperCollins, 1992.

Funk, Mary Margaret. *Tools Matter for Practicing the Spiritual Life.* New York: Continuum, 2001.

Greer, Ronald J. *If You Know Who You Are, You Will Know What to Do: Living with Integrity.* Nashville: Abingdon, 2009.

Gula, S. S., Richard M. *To Walk Together Again: The Sacrament of Reconciliation.* Ramsey, NJ: Paulist, 1984.

Hahn, Celia Allison. *Growing in Authority, Relinquishing Control: A New Approach to Faithful Leadership.* Herndon, VA: Alban Institute, 1994.

Harnish, James A. *Strength for the Broken Places.* Nashville: Abingdon, 2009.

Hauser, Richard J. *Moving in the Spirit: Becoming a Contemplative in Action.* Mahwah, NJ: Paulist, 1986.

Heschel, Abraham J. *Between God and Man: An Interpretation of Judaism.* New York: Free Press, 1997.

———. *I Asked for Wonder: A Spiritual Anthology.* Edited by Samuel H. Dresner. New York: Crossroad, 1993.

Hinson, E. Glenn. *Spiritual Preparation for Christian Leadership.* Nashville: Upper Room, 1999.

Howell, James C. *The Beautiful Work of Learning to Pray: 31 Lessons.* Nashville: Abingdon, 2003.

———. *The Kiss of God: 27 Lessons on the Holy Spirit.* Nashville: Abingdon, 2004.

Job, Rueben P. *40 Days with Wesley: A Daily Devotional Journey.* Nashville: Abingdon, 2017.

———. *A Guide to Retreat for All God's Shepherds*. Nashville: Abingdon, 1994.

———. *A Guide to Spiritual Discernment*. Nashville: Upper Room, 1996.

———. *A Journey Toward Solitude and Community*. Nashville: Upper Room Books, 1992.

———. *A Wesleyan Spiritual Reader*. Nashville: Abingdon, 1998.

———. *Becoming a Praying Congregation: Churchwide Leadership Tools*. Nashville: Abingdon, 2009.

———. *Life Stories*. Nashville: Abingdon, 2010.

———. *Listen: Praying in a Noisy World*. Nashville: Abingdon, 2014.

———. *Three Simple Questions: Knowing the God of Love, Hope, and Purpose*. Nashville: Abingdon, 2011.

———. *Three Simple Rules: A Wesleyan Way of Living*. Nashville: Abingdon, 2007.

Johnson, Ben Campbell. *GodSpeech: Putting Divine Disclosures into Human Words*. Grand Rapids: Eerdmans, 2006.

Johnson, Elizabeth A. *Consider Jesus: Waves of Renewal in Christology*. New York: Crossroad, 1990.

Johnson, Luke Timothy. *The Creed: What Christians Believe and Why It Matters*. New York: Doubleday, 2003.

Jordan-Lake, Joy. *Why Jesus Makes Me Nervous: Ten Alarming Words of Faith*. Brewster, MA: Paraclete, 2007.

Kadlecek, Jo. *Woman Overboard: How Passion Saved My Life*. Nashville: Fresh Air Books, 2009.

Kasper, Walter. *Jesus the Christ*. Mahwah, NJ: Paulist, 1976.

Keating, Thomas. *Invitation to Love: The Way of Christian Contemplation*. Rockport, MA: Element, 1992.

———. *Open Mind, Open Heart: The Contemplative Dimension of the Gospel*. 20th anniversary ed. New York: Continuum, 2006.

Kelly, Carole Marie. *Symbols of Inner Truth: Uncovering the Spiritual Meaning of Experience*. Mahwah, NJ: Paulist, 1988.

King, Martin Luther Jr. *A Testament of Hope: The Essential Writings of Martin Luther King Jr.* Edited by James M. Washington. New York: HarperCollins, 1986.

Kinnaman, David, and Gabe Lyons. *Unchristian: What a New Generation Really Thinks about Christianity . . . and Why It Matters.* Grand Rapids: Baker, 2007.

Kornfield, Jack. *A Path with Heart: A Guide Through the Perils and Promises of Spiritual Life.* New York: Bantam, 1993.

Langford, Thomas A. *Practical Divinity: Theology in the Wesleyan Tradition.* Vol. 1. Nashville: Abingdon, 1998.

Lawrence, Brother. *The Practice of the Presence of God.* New Kensington, PA: Whitaker House, 1982.

Maloney, George A. *In Jesus We Trust.* Notre Dame, IN: Ave Maria Press, 1990.

Manning, Brennan. *A Glimpse of Jesus: The Stranger to Self-Hatred.* New York: HarperCollins, 2003.

———. *Abba's Child: The Cry of the Heart for Intimate Belonging.* Enlarged ed. Colorado Springs: NavPress, 2015.

———. *Ruthless Trust: The Ragamuffin's Path to God.* New York: HarperCollins, 2000.

———. *The Wisdom of Tenderness: What Happens When God's Fierce Mercy Transforms Our Lives.* New York: HarperCollins, 2002.

Messer, Donald E. *Contemporary Images of Christian Ministry.* Nashville: Abingdon, 1989.

Moltmann, Jürgen. "The Disarming Child." 308–320. *Watch for the Light: Readings for Advent and Christmas.* Walden, NY: Plough Publishing, 2001.

Muto, Susan. *Late Have I Loved Thee: The Recovery of Intimacy.* New York: Crossroad, 1995.

Niederauer, George H. *Precious as Silver: Imagining Your Life With God.* Notre Dame, IN: Ave Maria Press, 2004.

Norris, Kathleen. *Amazing Grace: A Vocabulary of Faith*. New York: Riverhead Books, 1999.

Nouwen, Henri J. M. *Here and Now: Living in the Spirit*. New York: Crossroad, 1994.

———. *Life of the Beloved: Spiritual Living in a Secular World*. New York: Crossroad, 1992.

———. *The Return of the Prodigal Son: A Story of Homecoming*. New York: Doubleday, 1992.

———. *The Wounded Healer: Ministry in Contemporary Society*. New York: Image, 1972.

Olivia, Max. *Free to Pray, Free to Love: Growing in Prayer and Compassion*. Notre Dame, IN: Ave Maria Press, 1994.

Pennington, M. Basil. *Seeking His Mind: 40 Meetings with Christ*. Brewster, MA: Paraclete, 2002.

Peterson, Eugene H. *Christ Plays in Ten Thousand Places: A Conversation in Spiritual Theology*. Grand Rapids: Eerdmans, 2005.

———. *Tell It Slant: A Conversation on the Language of Jesus in His Stories and Prayers*. Grand Rapids: Eerdmans, 2008.

Puls, Joan. *Seek Treasures in Small Fields: Everyday Holiness*. Mystic, CT: Twenty-third Publications, 1993.

Rogers, Frank, Jr. "Discernment." 103-116. *Practicing Our Faith: A Way of Life for a Searching People*. Edited by Dorothy C. Bass. San Francisco. Jossey-Bass, 1997.

Rohr, Richard. *Everything Belongs: The Gift of Contemplative Prayer*. New York: Crossroad, 2003.

Rupp, Joyce. *The Cup of Our Life: A Guide to Spiritual Growth*. Notre Dame, IN: Ave Maria Press, 1997.

Schnase, Robert. *Ambition in Ministry: Our Spiritual Struggle with Success, Achievement, and Competition*. Nashville: Abingdon, 1993.

Shannon, William H. *Seeds of Peace: Contemplation and Non-Violence*. New York: Crossroad, 1996.

Shawchuck, Norman, and Rueben P. Job. *A Guide to Prayer for All Who Seek God*. Nashville: Upper Room, 2006.

Smith, Huston. *The Soul of Christianity: Restoring the Great Tradition*. New York: HarperSanFrancisco, 2005.

Soughers, Tara. *Treasures of Darkness: Finding God When Hope Is Hidden*. Nashville: Abingdon, 2009.

Steere, Douglas V. *Dimensions of Prayer*. New York: Women's Division, The General Board of Global Ministries, 1962.

Stevens, Becca. "Give Us This Day Our Daily Bread." 83–86. *Becoming a Praying Congregation: Churchwide Leadership Tools*, Rueben P. Job, Nashville: Abingdon, 2009.

———. *Hither & Yon: A Travel Guide for the Spiritual Journey*. Nashville: Dimensions for Living, 2007.

Taylor, Barbara Brown. *An Altar in the World: A Geography of Faith*. New York: HarperOne, 2009.

Teresa, Mother. *A Simple Path*. New York: Ballantine, 1995.

The Women of Magdalene with Becca Stevens. *Find Your Way Home: Words from the Street, Wisdom from the Heart*. Nashville: Abingdon, 2008.

Thomas à Kempis, *The Imitation of Christ*, contemporary text by William C. Creasy. Notre Dame, IN: Ave Maria Press, 2004.

Thompson, Marjorie J. *Family: The Forming Center*. Nashville: Upper Room Books, 1989.

Ulanov, Ann and Barry. *Primary Speech: A Psychology of Prayer*. Atlanta: John Knox, 1982.

Underhill, Evelyn. *The Ways of the Spirit*. New York: Crossroad, 1993.

Vanier, Jean. *Jesus, the Gift of Love*. New York: Crossroad, 1994.

Vennard, Jane E. *A Praying Congregation: The Art of Teaching Spiritual Practice*. Herndon, VA: The Alban Institute, 2005.

Wesley, John. *A Collection of Prayers for Families.* Available online: http://wesley.nnu.edu/john-wesley/christian-library/a-christian-library-volume-12/a-collection-of-prayers-for-families/.

———. "The Use of Money," *The Works of John Wesley*, Vol. 2, The Works of John Wesley. Edited by Albert C. Outler. Nashville: Abingdon Press, 1985.

Wicks, Robert J. *Everyday Simplicity: A Practical Guide to Spiritual Growth.* Notre Dame, IN: Sorin Books, 2000.

———. *Touching the Holy: Ordinariness, Self-Esteem, and Friendship.* Notre Dame, IN: Ave Maria Press, 1992.

Wiederkehr, Macrina. *A Tree Full of Angels: Seeing the Holy in the Ordinary.* New York: HarperOne, 2009.

Willard, Dallas. *The Divine Conspiracy: Rediscovering Our Hidden Life in God.* New York: HarperCollins, 1998.

Williams, Clifford. *Singleness of Heart: Restoring the Divided Soul.* Grand Rapids: Eerdmans, 1994.

Willimon, William H. "The Messiness of Ministry." *Princeton Seminary Bulletin* 14 (1993): 229–233.

Wolpert, Daniel. *Leading a Life With God: The Practice of Spiritual Leadership.* Nashville: Upper Room Books, 2006.

Wuellner, Flora Slosson. *Heart of Healing, Heart of Light: Encountering God, Who Shares and Heals Our Pain.* Nashville: Upper Room, 1992.

Lectionary Guide

You may prefer to use *When You Pray* while observing the Christian year. The following list suggests which weeks of *When You Pray* align with the Sundays of Advent, Lent, and Easter, as well as other important liturgical days such as Epiphany and Pentecost.

Note that because the dates of Easter and Lent vary from year to year, there may be more than eight Sundays between Epiphany (Week 6 below) and Transfiguration Sunday (Week 15). You may account for this difference by choosing one or more of the ordinary Sundays between Weeks 30 and 52 to read in this interval in addition to Weeks 7–14. Regardless of the year, Week 15 should always be read on Transfiguration Sunday, the Sunday before Lent begins. Week 52 should always be read on Christ the King Sunday, the week before Advent begins.

If you do choose to follow the Christian year, you may wish to substitute the included printed Scripture passages each week with those listed in the Revised Common Lectionary. The readings from the Revised Common Lectionary for the current year may be found at www.textweek.com, where you will also find a complete listing of every passage for each week of church year A, B, or C.

First Sunday of Advent	Week 1	12/1/19	11/29/20
Second Sunday of Advent	Week 2		
Third Sunday of Advent	Week 3		
Fourth Sunday of Advent	Week 4		12/20
First Sunday after Christmas	Week 5		12/27

Epiphany Sunday	Week 6	1|5
Transfiguration Sunday	Week 15	2|23
First Sunday in Lent	Week 16	3|1
Second Sunday in Lent	Week 17	
Third Sunday in Lent	Week 18	
Fourth Sunday in Lent	Week 19	
Fifth Sunday in Lent	Week 20	
Palm/Passion Sunday	Week 21	4|5
Easter Sunday	Week 22	4|12
Second Sunday of Easter	Week 23	
Third Sunday of Easter	Week 24	
Fourth Sunday of Easter	Week 25	
Fifth Sunday of Easter	Week 26	
Sixth Sunday of Easter	Week 27	
Seventh Sunday of Easter	Week 28	5|24
Pentecost Sunday	Week 29	5|31
Trinity Sunday	Week 30	6|7
Christ the King Sunday	Week 52	11|22